WITCH BOTTLES
HISTORY, CULTURE, MAGIC

WITCH BOTTLES
History, Culture, Magic

DANIEL HARMS

PUBLISHED BY AVALONIA
WWW.AVALONIABOOKS.COM

PUBLISHED BY AVALONIA

BM AVALONIA
LONDON
WC1N 3XX
ENGLAND, UK

WWW.AVALONIABOOKS.COM

WITCH BOTTLES: HISTORY, CULTURE, MAGIC

COPYRIGHT © DANIEL HARMS, 2020

ISBN: 978-1-910191-00-2
(PAPERBACK)

FIRST EDITION, OCTOBER 2022

COVER ART BY EMILY CARDING, 2022

ILLUSTRATIONS BY HELOISA SAILLE, 2021

DESIGNED AND PRODUCED BY AVALONIA LTD
BM AVALONIA, LONDON, WC1N 3XX, UNITED KINGDOM
WWW.AVALONIABOOKS.COM

ALL RIGHTS RESERVED.

British Library Cataloguing in Publication Data. A catalogue record for this book is available from the British Library.

Every effort has been made to credit material to, and obtain permission from, copyright holders for the use of their work. If you notice any error or omission please notify the publisher so that corrections can be incorporated into future editions of this work. The information provided in this book hopes to inspire and inform. The author and publisher assume no responsibility for the effects, or lack thereof, obtained from the practices described in this book.

The reproduction of any part of this book, other than for review purposes, is strictly forbidden, in all formats, without the prior written consent of Avalonia Ltd and the copyright holders.

Acknowledgements

Thanks to Ben Fernee for requesting this book to begin with, and for nurturing it into its first appearance. Thanks to Nick Crane for providing access to a crucial report, and to Richard Powell and the interlibrary loan staff at the State University of New York at Cortland for a continuing flow of valuable information. Both Kresen Kernow and Dr. M. Chris Manning gave much-appreciated permission to quote from their materials. Others who proved invaluable include the staff at the Folger Shakespeare Library, the Museum of Witchcraft and Magic at Boscastle, the Pennsylvania German Cultural Heritage Center, the Society of Antiquaries of London, the Preston Park Museum, the Louth Museum, the Royal Institute of British Architects Drawings and Archives Collections, and the Saffron Walden Museum. Also, my thanks and apologies to all those who assisted but whom I have forgotten.

Table of Contents

Unsettling the Contents: A Foreword on Witch Bottles
  by *Alexander Cummins*   11

Introduction   21
The Witch in Belief, Folklore, and Medical Practice   23
Origins of the Witch Bottle   28
Witch Bottles in Scandinavia   65
Witch Bottles in North America   67
Today's Witch Bottles   82
Witch Bottles in the Media   86

Discussion   88
Conclusion   99

Works Consulted   101
Index   113

A Note on the Text

When writing this book, I chose to arrange the material chronologically. This works well for material such as court cases, newspaper articles, and other written sources, but it does tend to skew for archaeological sources and others where dating is more questionable. I've tried to work in the latter material in the places it seems best, but the chronology of these items is often open to debate.

Unsettling the Contents
A Foreword on Witch Bottles
by *Alexander Cummins*

The unearthed witch-bottle is something of a murky treasure. Sealed and secreted, they encapsulate magical ideas and sorcerous strategies for undoing the blights of bewitchment. Such strategies are a far cry from ennobling cleansing or sanctifying purifications, instead launching counter-offensive harm against the cursing witch through manipulation of the patient's urine: specifically, by boiling and/or burying it away with sharp objects. Such ritual items invite consideration as tangible evidence not only of spiritual concerns, anxieties, and ideals, but of spiritual actions – to protect, to reverse, to remediate.

Perhaps unsurprisingly for a practice involving pins and thorns and such 'stinking waters', witch-bottling was considered morally dubious by its critics: a species of resorting to witchcraft to deal with witchcraft. Even those confident their witch-bottling was justified frequently deployed and activated them specifically by concealing them in secret for their unimpeded continual operation. As such, study of these ritual items and their occasionally furtive uses is especially helpfully assisted by methodologies of material history and archaeology, for with proper care against talking over the evidence with speculation or flatlining distinct practices and approaches, we may come to some considerable insights into humans and their magics.

It might surprise even interested parties that definitive works on witch-bottles are a little rare on the ground. The present work includes a helpful bibliography of course; however this apparent scarcity is perhaps more understandable once we grasp that witch-bottles are not static or fixed in either their historical contexts or their occult conceptions. The term 'witch-bottle' itself has been a debated – even contentious – one. Some find it an overly broad label for each and every ritual act of secreting away containers, inviting too many disparate practices to its homogenising feast. To others it is an extinguishably narrow term that unhelpfully excludes all but a tiny fraction of historical objects bounded to and by a specific region and period.

Enter Daniel Harms' present survey, carefully laying out the evidence and arguments; not merely to point at controversies but to better elucidate and illuminate the material and sharpen our very means of its analysis. The crux of the present thesis – in its methodological execution and in its valuable contribution to the field of study – is in explicitly approaching the witch-bottle as ritual assemblage: specifically as the ritual assemblage of container, sharp objects, and urine.

As any historian of early modern magic and humoural theory will tell you, urine was considered a bodily *ex-pression* of the excreted dross of gross blood and its corrupted humours. It has thus long been apprehended as a medium to consider for signs of imbalance in popular medical diagnostic techniques of uroscopy. In the experiments of the witch bottles, a 'grieved' victim's urine is further employed as a means and material to actually effect a return to health. In the marks of *maleficia* that might be beheld in the chamber-pot could also be located a magical signature which could be traced back to its malevolent sender.

Proper treatment must of course deal with the underlying cause of the malady and suffering not simply its symptoms after all. In these unbewitching treatments, the ultimate cause to be dealt with was generally (the body of) the witch themselves. Such bottle operations seem to use urine to reverse the magical link formed by the assault of the spiritual assailant. Urine is weaponised to *'spoil the witch'* as it is put in certain unwitching cants. Ultimately this counter-offense-as-the-best-defense intends to restore the victim's balanced health by neutralising their attacker. Whether by high-flame boil or earthy entombment, these bottles burn up and or seal away the witch's poisons lacing the patient's waters by the pins of retaliation and the conjurations of containment and expulsion.

In exploring these very operations and operators, this present book has much to recommend it to students, scholars, and practitioners. In the name of brevity I will outline two main contributions: to the historical and historiographical contexts for how to think *about* witch-bottles; and to the conceptual and technical occult philosophy and magical practices of thinking (and acting) *with* witch-bottles.

HISTORICAL CONTEXTS

This study firstly offers a historical survey of considerable aid in better understanding these objects and their traditions. The author has collated several distinct yet interrelated types of evidence: written instructions for constructing and deploying witch-bottles; witch trial accounts of their employment; and the customs and beliefs recorded by folklorists and antiquarians concerning making and using these ritual objects. Each of these types of sources offer their own insights and require their own contexts and methodological considerations which the present work communicates clearly and fairly.

Such careful historiographical analyses and interpretation which accompanies the assessment of the historical record also assists in acknowledging both the value of archaeological data and the occasional limitations of archaeological means – especially to approach actions and practices like ritual magic – in the face of the wrack and ruin of time's erosions upon the objects of our study. The present monograph is informed by examination of the material history, and includes synopsis of such pertinent details as: the trade and reception of bellarmine vessels; and the appearance of iron witch-bottles in the nineteenth century, noting the deadly damages – not to mention dramatic appeal – of their habit of exploding with particularly destructive ferocity when heated.

An intellectual history of witch-bottle theory – addressing the accounts and analysis of witch-bottling procedures by thinkers and doctors such as Joseph Blagrave – is combined with a wealth of excerpted case reports of stopping up urine, bewitchment, and counter-magic. This present survey offers stories of the cunning of the gun-wielding white witch of Zennor, Aunt Maggey, and of the unbewitching practices of Dr Bourn of Southwark, Dr Hainks of Spitalfields, old Cunning Murrell, and of course the formularies and experiments of the cunning galvanist William Dawson Bellhouse, along with countless unnamed local folk magicians, wise women, and conjuring doctors. In so doing, we trace the works of various types of historical practitioners – from Paracelsian 'Chymists' to cunning-folk and even charlatan quacks – through their engagement with the experiments and effects of such bottles.

This present study also connects up expressions of witch-bottling from England and the Germanic lands of central Europe with the customs and cunning of Scandinavia. If the details of the prosecution and eventual acquittal of Jørgen Larsen of Nørre Lyndelse parish discussed are anything to go by, Danish sorcerers of the late nineteenth century certainly sealed and buried personal concerns for rites of healing. A Norwegian operation from 1830 employing more modern equipment nevertheless confirms that even when done primarily to heal there is still an evil to remove. Anti-witching shades of hot compelling work remain, as it is said 'the person who did the evil will come and ask you to remove the kettle from the stove because it burns him, but you must not remove it until he has made the diseased person well again or given advice that you can use.'

Such global comparisons also span witch-bottling in the New World, and this survey includes an account of the early modern transatlantic cunning of Hannah Weacome of Boston, as well as incensed reports condemning the practice by Increase Mather and minister of Salem Village Deodat Lawson. Salem's own witch trials also included mention of the practice, and the confession of Martha Emerson is also considered. Finally, analysis of North American witch-bottles in the modern age is collated geographically, highlighting regional specificities and variations, intersections with other folk magic traditions such as the powwow of the Pennsylvania Dutch, as well as providing further data points for charting lines of transmission of the practices.

MAGICAL CONCEPTS

The second set of contributions worth highlighting in this foreword concern the conceptual and technical considerations that help us not only think about but work with witch bottles. Wading into the mass of ideas about what they are, how they work, and what counts (and what doesn't count) as a witch-bottle, this survey spends no time constructing or defending a dogmatic thesis. Instead these careful assessments work to refine analysis of the various similarities and differences between conceptions and expressions of this particular species of apotropaic container experiments we call "witch bottles".

Study of what the author carefully frames as 'variations on the elements of witch bottles' begin with comparative and contrasting examples of wider global ward-burial practices: from Middle Eastern "demon bowls" to the clay vessels found beneath thresholds in Germany and the Netherlands. The present work notes evidences of various operations involving urine and pins (or similar sharp metal objects) which provide wider context for magical understandings of such implements and the practices employing them. As such, this treatise accounts for both the Paracelsian 'urinary experiments' of the seventeenth century and some older apotropaic operations against witches, imps, and the malefic dead. Time and again, we see the interplay of protocols and procedures employing closed containers and those using open heating vessels (such as pans or pots) informing each other. This survey also notes the limitations and lacunas of such evidences in appropriately cautioning against unhelpfully eliding differing ideas and actions. Through assessing these particularities of witch-bottling the present work offers particular analysis of how more passive protective warding functions intersect with the active counter-offense of reversal operations.

Variations of additional required materials are carefully noted: from the various specifications concerning animal hearts, into which those pins, needles, thorns, and nails are frequently stuck, to short written charms and versicles; and from extra personal concerns, especially locks of hair and nail parings, to inclusions of fabrics – sometimes themselves heart-shaped – as well as diverse other ingredients such as sulphur, salt, (animal) blood, (human) teeth, dragonsblood, and other 'mysterious powders'. Its survey of the sites of internment and exhumation of such bottles – covering burials under churches, secreted away in corners of town halls, planted in graves, up chimneys, at wayside crosses, and beneath parish boundary walls – illuminates the variety of efficacious deployments for such objects.

We also learn that, despite prevalent logics of witch spoiling, engagements with the attacker varied considerably: from accounts of practitioners scrying the foam of the urine boiling over the fire in order to see the very face of the assailing witch, to more medical-looking client-focused procedures of neutralising a merely anonymous attacker. Certainly the practices of boiling the urine and pins and so on *in order to* locate the witch – forcing them to reveal themselves either by being physically drawn to the work or simply by their screams of pain – highlight significant social and interpersonal complexities of the intra-community tensions created by witchcraft accusations made public through such counter-magical means.

Varying ideas about what and how exactly the witch is affected by the bottle are also considered: from disempowerment of their curses to causing the attacker bodily harm, dysfunction, and enfeeblement. Some accounts claim their bottle stops the witch urinating, and that this itself could be fatal. It was said by some that the pins in the bottle prick the witch's heart. Protracted or especially severe bottle workings are often thought to visit maddening levels of pain and even outright death upon the witch.

This present study also notes a turn in the late nineteenth century to use and adapt witch bottle technologies for spells of other specific works of compulsion, such as the bottle operation advised to Deborah Wood by Adelina Westernoff in 1888 to force the absent father of her child to return. Another reported operation, from Brierley and dated to 1894 – in which a jilted lover attempted to compel her wandering boyfriend back to her – seems to confirm an underlying logic whereby the (usually counter-offensive) damage of the witch-bottles' pins was employed for typical erotic malefic ends: to torture the literal target of the operator's affections to not rest or enjoy anything until they come crawling back. The bottle of unbewitching even seems to haunt a Cornish operation of curing warts by touching pins to them before they are bottled, sealed, and buried. That this bottle is to be buried at a crossroads or new grave further highlights the variety of engagements with the potent loci of these spiritual ecologies that such operations may require beyond attending to the thresholds of home and the heart of the hearth.

Cases involving animals are also included in the present study, with careful attention paid to their regimens' adherences to and departures from the standards, procedures, and customs of treating human victims of witchcraft. It seems horses were especially prone to being targeted, perhaps unsurprisingly given their value and importance in pre-modern life.

The operative necessity of ritual silence is also noted several times in witch-bottling accounts. There seem various key moments in the processes reported – typically when seething the waters and especially when quenching red hot iron into it – at which even 'a single word mars the whole charm'. Beyond silence itself as a ritual protocol (never mind a sensible act of self-preservation when doing magic) these instructions further highlight that such operations were sometimes considered to require delicacy, care, and great attention.

VOLATILE VESSELS

In apprehending these contexts and concepts we may come to better consider beliefs, customs, and understandings of the magics and the meanings of witch-bottles from the early modern period to the present day. Through the encapsulating lens of the witch-bottle this work offers reflections upon broader and deeper shifting legal definitions of magic, poison, and harm; as well as the changing economic, cultural, and intellectual circumstances of communities and attendant historical turns and responses in social mores, tensions, expectations, and practices. We also observe a range of continuities of practice in these eddying shifts in emphasis and circumstance swirling in this particular looking-glass.

In getting to the bottom of the witch-bottle this study traces pertinent influences informing variegated dynamic expressions of such ritual objects and diagnoses how these ideas and actions vie and intertwine throughout not only the constellated historical record of evidences, but in the working-books curated and the ritual acts of conjuration performed by the practitioners who made experiment of them.

Alexander Cummins
New England, 2021

Introduction

This book was initially published as part of a slipcased set by the Society of Esoteric Endeavour, accompanying a reproduction of the notebook of the nineteenth-century Liverpool cunning man William Dawson Bellhouse. Publisher Ben Fernee asked me to write two small books covering two sets of magical operations in Bellhouse's grimoire. At the urging of readers unable to obtain the set, I decided to update and re-release the witch bottle notebook.

In recent years, more people have become aware of the existence and significance of witch bottles, leading to more discoveries and creations. Tracking down many of these accounts is taxing for the casual reader and takes considerable effort for even specialists. Thus, my goal here is to be comprehensive, giving enough details that scholars might track down many cases of interest, while providing sufficient anecdotes and examples of incantations and the like for those seeking such things.

My own background is a librarian and a student of texts on ritual magic, who had some slight training in archaeology from years ago. Experts are sure to disagree with some of my interpretations. I would encourage readers to seek out the works in the bibliography to balance my own perspectives.

Throughout this book, I make heavy and perhaps careless use of words such as 'magic,' 'magician,' and 'supernatural.' This might reflect modern sensibilities more than those of the people who utilized these items in past circumstances. Indeed, no contemporary documentation accompanies most discovered bottles, and we have few hints as to the philosophies that underlay the practice. From what accounts survive, however, they seem based in the belief that one person may affect another person, creature, or object through non-physical and invisible means, and that manipulation of physical items, possibly including ritual statements and actions, might lead to its reverse. Such ideas might be placed under different labels in different periods, and we should be cognizant that these labels did and do have considerable weight upon people's lives.

Daniel Harms
2021

The Witch in Belief, Folklore, and Medical Practice

Throughout history, people encountered a variety of misfortunes: illness, accidents, failed crops, sick animals, poor weather, fires, thefts, and many others. Today, many of us have access to government and charitable programs, police, fire departments, health care systems for both humans and animals, and insurance. All of these were rudimentary at best in past eras, leaving many people living a precarious existence in which any one problem could cascade to destroy a household.

What would cause these misfortunes? Some disasters would affect an entire community, but others just one household, leaving the rest untouched. Sometimes the cause was clearly manifest – a hailstorm, an invading army – but others had no perceptible cause. Different societies attribute such troubles to gods and spirits, but others blame witches, dangerous individuals secretly using supernatural powers to inflict injury on those who displeased them.

Readers might have different reactions to this word; indeed, some might self-identify themselves as witches and feel uncomfortable with the negative associations that attach to it. Such associations are hard to avoid, given the term's lengthy connection to negative behaviours which are entwined around the traditional milieu of the "witch bottle." Thus, my use of "witch" in this book will be largely based on this definition, simply for the sake of clarity, not as a dismissal of other definitions of the term.

If the accounts of European witch trials are any indication, many of those accused of being witches did not attempt supernatural harm. Nonetheless, if a society believes that witches exist, some people will exploit those beliefs to gain power and concessions from those around them. Given the effect of mind and belief on the body, such efforts might result in actual harm in some circumstances. This is not to justify witchcraft accusations or the consequences thereof, yet the willingness of some individuals to play the role of witches has played a part in the continuation of such beliefs.

In societies that believe in witches, people often seek protection and remedy against their powers. Although the witch trials were horrific, they only flared up sporadically, often when and where broader social stressors were already in play. People suspecting witchcraft usually relied on less formal ways to help themselves, sometimes working with neighbours, local clerics, or specialists in supernatural remedies.

People seeking to drive off witchcraft might draw on an array of supernatural solutions. For example, "bleeding" a witch – often by striking them on the face in such a way as to draw blood – was seen as a means of causing the reversal of a spell. Secular authorities discouraged such violence, so less confrontational practices were more common. Those who feared witchcraft could wear amulets, or seek the blessing of their homes and property, or perform other charms, including hanging up herbs or horseshoes, inserting red-hot objects into cursed butter churns, or filling an animal heart with pins. In a small portion of northwest Europe, the creation of witch bottles served the same purpose.

WHAT ARE WITCH BOTTLES?

The term "witch bottle" appeared in a catalogue for the Saffron Walden Museum**Error! Bookmark not defined.** in Essex, in 1845, referring briefly to an item on display. After so many years, no one knows what exactly that item was.

For our purposes, I will refer to a "witch bottle" as a ritual assemblage, usually intended to fight off maleficent magic, that employs at least two of the following three ingredients: a bottle, urine, and sharp objects, which may include needles, pins, or thorns. The "ritual" component here should be taken to mean a purpose with a non-material component. For example, a jar a carpenter uses to hold their nails would not qualify. Urine and sharp objects need not be all that is included, and many assemblages may have components beyond these. If some ambiguity exists about the presence of these items due to preservation, the presence of two, or the positioning of the bottle, might be factors to be considered.

Another common definition of the witch bottle incorporates the location in which it was discovered, usually indicating that it was hidden somewhere around a household. Without either of the other two physical elements, however, a discovered bottle embroils us in questions about how we can determine whether a bottle was deliberately concealed, or the purpose of the concealment based upon context, condition, and association with other objects. I have most omitted such discoveries, and I'm sure some readers will disagree. Nonetheless, I feel that maintaining a focus on less debatable examples is more valuable – and these are in no short supply.

Folklore and magical practice also refer to bottles that hold a spirit or witch. Reports of these objects date considerably earlier and over a greater geographic range, so these will only be noted in the few instances when they seem to overlap with the definition above.

Once assembled, the bottle's creator either places it into a fire or disposes of it by burying it or throwing it into water. This is only the beginning of our understanding, as the nature, usage, contents, placement, and other aspects of these bottles differ considerably among the accounts and surviving artefacts.

TYPES OF EVIDENCE

Although witch bottles had been reported for hundreds of years, no serious attempt to examine them seems to have been made until Ralph Merrifield's work in the Fifties. The evidence assembled since then can be placed into four categories, each with its strengths and challenges.

The first category consists of written prescriptions for the creation of these bottles. These recipes provide details on the creation of the bottles not present in other sources. Nonetheless, we might ask how often these specific prescriptions were used, or if they were recorded for practice or simply for curiosity. It is likely that these few written fragments are only part of a broader tradition that was either unwritten or lost.

Accounts of witch trials fall into the second category. Notably, those conducting the trials rarely prosecuted people for the creation of these bottles. The use of witch bottles was a frowned-upon but often efficacious means by which people could attempt to protect themselves from witchcraft. On the other hand, we have few actual trial records describing them. The gap is filled with authors writing sensationalist pamphlets about the trials, who might not have cared much for accuracy.

Third, we have the accounts of folklorists describing witch bottle beliefs and objects. Such collectors, mostly working in the nineteenth and early twentieth centuries, had their own interests, emphases, and biases. One key concern is the likelihood that some folklorists, catering to their readers' sensibilities, omitted references to urine as an ingredient or referred to it as "water" or other euphemisms, as this ingredient does not turn up often in such works.

Finally, we have the surviving witch bottles uncovered at sites on two continents, mostly over the last century. Although these artefacts are some of our best indicators of actual practice, they themselves do not constitute a complete record of the practices. Placing a bottle in a fire to burst would have left little remaining evidence that could be distinguished from ordinary broken stoneware or glassware. Some ritual aspects – verbal charms, ritual timing, or silence, for instance – reported solely in the written record would leave no archaeological trace. The first response of most people when finding an intriguing antique bottle is to pick it up and pour out the contents, a reaction to which even archaeologists are prone[1]. The first formal laboratory analysis of such a bottle was conducted in 2009, opening the door to further investigation of these artefacts and their creation[2]. Still, some substances included in the bottle might not be detectable due to the material not surviving or the lack of tests for detection.

---

1 Kelly, "Witch Bottles."
2 Massey, "Field Note." Pitts, "Urine to Navel Fluff."

Origins of the Witch Bottle

Around the year 300 BC, two or more individuals in Athens undertook a magical ceremony. They purchased a miniature stew pot, of a type often used for funerary offerings. After painting a red ochre wreath pattern around the middle, they etched dozens of personal names – men and women, local and foreign - into the sides of the pot. Inside they placed the head and feet of a chicken, the parts of the bird with the least amount of meat. A doornail transfixed the pot, puncturing the base, and a coin, later corroded beyond recognition, was placed over the pot's mouth. Our mysterious creators then buried the whole item beneath the floor of a sculptor's studio near the Agora.[3]

Would this be considered a witch bottle? I would argue against this. Even if we set aside its distance in space and time from the other examples, the many names etched into the ceramics suggest that this is a spell intended for judicial or political purposes, likely against those working in the building under which it was buried. This is very much unlike the witch bottles, which were usually interpreted as reversing hostile magic, not perpetuating it. Our Greek grouping includes many items similar to those used for funeral rituals, and its main parallels from the period are the "saucer pyres," buried protective assemblages consisting of tiny ceramics and burned items, commonly employed at the time. The example should encourage us to look beyond our initial impressions to find the differences and nuances in the material.

There has been some recent debate as to whether the term "witch bottles" is accurate, and whether it is more helpful to

---

3 Lamont, "The Curious Case of the Cursed Chicken."

refer to it as a "urinary experiment," arising from late seventeenth-century Paracelsian procedures that later became incorporated into procedures against hostile magic. The previous century, however, provides us with a wide variety of anti-witchcraft rituals using a mixture of our three components, often in contexts where they would not be obvious to archaeological discovery.[4]

At least one scholar has drawn parallels with practices from Germany and the Netherlands in which people buried clay pots and jugs below the thresholds of their houses. Often placed upside down, these ceramics might be empty or contain eggshells, coins, bones, ash, or other items. These items might reflect early practices involving foundation sacrifices, either being placed to trap evil spirits or to hold the good fortune of the household. The placement of a vessel is interesting, but the sharp objects and liquid are not reported as present.[5]

Another precursor to the witch bottle charms could be a procedure in which urine and iron objects are boiled in a pot or pan. One such charm appears in Folger Manuscript V.b.26, dating to the last decades of the sixteenth century. The author wrote the instructions for the charm in a simple cipher, which can be rendered as follows:

> *Take the urine of the party that is bewitched and seethe it in a pot, close covered. Then take a pigeon heart, and stick five needles in it, and set with the urine till the urine be consumed, saying as is above written.*[6]

---

4 Thwaite, "What Is a 'Witch Bottle'?."
5 Hänselmann, "Die Vergrabenen und Eingemauerten Thongeschirre des Mittelalters"; Merrifield, "Witch Bottles and Magical Jugs." The tradition bears similarities to the incantation bowls of the Middle East, in which inverted bowls were placed beneath the foundations of houses. For a summary of the research, see Bohak, *Ancient Jewish Magic*, 183–93. Given the lack of a clear chronological or geographical connection between the practices, however, we should be cautious about linking the two.
6 Folger MS. V.b.26, 223. The spelling here and in other manuscript sources has been modernized. This particular piece was copied by Frederick Hockley

The magician is to recite from the Gospel of St. John (likely the first chapter, which was often used in magical procedures) three times, and then say:

> *In the name of the Father, the Son, and the Holy Ghost, that even as this water and urine doth now waste, consume, and burn, so may his or hers [or] their witchcrafts, enchantments, sorcery, or charms which did or hath bewitched this person N., may presently by and by return and lighten upon themselves again, and to this I do charge you, by these names of God our Lord Jesus Christ, Tetragramaton, Alpha et Omega, Messias, Sother, Emanuell, Adonay, Algramay, Diagramay, Agla, Joth, Tetragram, Saday, by these names and by all other names, and by all other names of our Lord Jesus Christ, do I con[jure] you, that you do cause that even as this urine doth, &c.*[7]

One intriguing aspect of this charm is the inclusion of an animal heart, which is absent or replaced with a cloth heart in many later accounts.

A manuscript compilation of alchemical and medical experiments includes a seventeenth-century charm to overcome witchcraft in a similar vein:

> *Take the party's water grieved, and set it on the fire, and put into it a little sulfur. Then read the Gospel of St. John for Christmas Day three times, and when the urine doth begin to boil, have in a readiness three needles, and in putting them into the urine one after another, you must say in putting in the first, you must say [sic], "One in God's name," in putting in the second, say, "Two in God's name," and so for the third, say, "Three in God's name." Then say, "In the name of the Father, of the Son, and of the Holy Ghost. Amen. Even as this urine doth waste, consume, and burn, so may his, her, or their witchcrafts, enchantments, or sorceries, or any other which hath bewitched N., may return and light upon themselves again, and that by the most virtuous names*

---

into his Occult Spells notebook dated to 1829. Hockley and Manus, *Occult Spells*, 50.
7 Ibid. See parallels in Additional MS. 36,674, 145.

> *of God, Tetragrammaton, Alpha et Omega, Messias, Sother, Emanuel, Unigenitus, Vita, Via, Jesus Christus, Amen. By these holy names of God, I drive and curse thee, and swear you from your office and dignity. I do drive you by the virtue of them into the nether pit of hellfire, there to remain and burn with unquenchable fire, till the day of judgment, and precept that you do cause that, even as this urine doth waste, consume, and burn, so may his, her, or their witchcraft that hath bewitched N. thy servant return this three times over," and at every time say our Lord's Prayer. And at the same hour and time that the prayer is said, an alteration shall be in the party bewitched, and so by God's grace it shall mend afterwards*[8]

A contemporary account appears in Reverend George Gifford's *A Dialogue concerning Witches*, from 1593. The Reverend describes one technique common to a "cunning man," or local magical practitioner, as follows:

> *the cunning man biddeth set on a posnet*[9] *or some pan with nails, and seethe them, and the witch shall come in while they be in seething, and within a few dates after, her face will be all bescratched with the nails. And I have heard that some old woman coming in, her face hath indeed been as it were scratched within a few days after, for the shingles or such like break forth.*[10]

We have one archaeological find that might pertain to this practice: an iron bowl containing bent pins found in a stream near Northampton. The item could date to any time between the sixteenth and the eighteenth centuries, however, and no other material in witch bottles has turned up inside – although given the circumstances in which it was found, this is hardly surprising.[11]

---

8 Sloane 3706, 23r.
9 *Posnet*: A metal pot with three feet and a handle.
10 Gifford et al., *A Dialogue Concerning Witches and Witchcraft*, f. G2 v., G3 r. Spelling has been modernized.
11 Brindle, "Record ID: NARC-0ACAB1 - POST MEDIEVAL Witch Bottle."

Such charms were not confined to this place and time. We have one example from Germany in 1562, in which a clergyman sought to stop witchcraft by boiling a patient's nails and urine in a pan.[12] On February 16, 1654, Ann Greene was accused of witchcraft at York. She responded that she was a healer specializing in a few techniques. One of these was to take the urine and a lock of hair from a headache sufferer, to boil them, and finally to burn them in a fire. She made no mention of witches being responsible for the headache, however.[13]

A similar charm was recorded in the notebook of the eighteenth-century Yorkshire cunning man Timothy Crowther:

> *Take hair of each quarter, some of each hoof and horn, sew it up in a cloth, and in the form of a ball; prick it full of pins and put in 3 needles. Boil it in the afflicted water till the pan be like to burn, then throw it into the fire and say (three times)* — *"Witch, witch, witch, thus shalt thou burn in hell." Take care that no body come in the house all the time you are in doing of it; it must be done three times at the change, full, and quarter.*[14]

In 1843, Charlotte Horn of Plymstock was deeply concerned about the health of her mother, Ann. Agnes Hill of Plymouth offered to help her with many amulets and charms. In addition, Charlotte was to obtain "fasting water," a rooster, and ash wood from three different parishes. Once Charlotte brought these to Plymouth, a bloody rite began:

> *Hill then said, we must kill the cock, and desired her mother to cut its throat, which she did with a razor. The cock was held over the new earthen pan, holding the fasting water and the blood, which was mingled together, and then put over the fire to boil. Hill then cut open the cock and took out its heart, and told her mother to stick seven new pins into it, likewise seven new needles, and nine blackthorn prickles. The*

---

12 De Waardt, "From Cunning Man to Natural Healer."
13 Raine, *Depositions from the Castle of York*, 64–65.
14 Dawson, *History of Skipton: (W.R. Yorks.)*, 394.

ash wood was put on the fire under the pan, the heart was hung up to roast before the fire, and it was afterwards thrown into the fire, pins, needles, and all.

Although witchcraft is never mentioned by name, it seems this was the cause. Hill's other remedies went so far as burning every piece of the mother's furniture. The court in Plymouth fined her, and Hill had to flee the court due to angry locals.[15]

One Norfolk clergyman related a cure for any illness attributed to bewitchment. Two people must meet at midnight, with one person directing the other in complete silence. Nine nails, each one from a different horseshoe, must be combined with urine from the victim and boiled over the fire. This must continue until three, five, or seven nails – the more that move, the more difficult the case – move within the liquid, and the victim cries out. With that, the spirit will depart. On one occasion, a boy accompanying the rite was silent until the end, when he cried out when he saw something black exiting the room through a keyhole. The bewitched child did not recover.[16]

If we take these accounts as a model for later witch bottles, the use of a pot or pan that is not broken or buried might account for the lack of evidence of witch bottles before this time. In fact, a nineteenth-century charm discussed later may be pursued with either a pot and a bottle.

One final variation on the elements of a witch bottle appears in *De Cerebri Morbis* [Of the Diseases of the Brain], written by Jason Pratensis in 1549. Shortly before composing the book, a priest visited Pratensis with a curious problem. A woman appeared to visit him in the night, sitting on his chest so he could barely breathe. Seeking a solution, he went to an old woman, who advised him to urinate in his chamber pot at twilight and stop it up with the hose from his right leg. The

---

15 "Extraordinary Superstition at Plymouth."
16 Glyde, *Norfolk Garland*, 51–52.

witch responsible would visit him before the day was out. All this occurred as the woman had told him. Even though the witch's bladder could find no release, she nonetheless refused to free the priest from his torment. Eventually the doctor was able to convince him to pursue medical treatment, and he was cured.[17]

Notably, Pratensis was a physician living in Zierikzee, Holland, which means that this was a cure from across the Channel similar to the witch bottle. All it lacked to meet my requirements would be the sharp objects. Reginald Scot himself noted this case in his *Discoverie of Witchcraft* (1584), so learned individuals in England would have been aware of it.[18]

THE APPEARANCE OF WITCH BOTTLES

The first artefacts claimed to be witch bottles appear in the United Kingdom circa 1500. A lead stopper in the mouth of a stoneware container, found at a site in Kingston Lisle, bears the imprint of an Austro-Burgundian jeton, or a counter placed on a board to keep track of accounts, from 1482-1555.[19] A similar seal with the imprint of a jeton from Tournai dates to the late fifteenth century.[20] It is uncertain, based on the data presented on these items, why these are considered witch bottles.

The most compelling evidence of witch bottles themselves appears during the seventeenth century. We might begin with the famous account in Joseph Glanvil's *Saducismus Triumphatus* (1681), as told to William Brearly of Christ's College, Cambridge. He had been staying in Suffolk around 1640, when he learned of his landlady's brush with witchcraft.

---

17 Pratensis, *De Cerebri Morbis*, 408–9.
18 Pestronk, "The First Neurology Book"; Scot, *The Discoverie of Witchcraft*, 83–84.
19 Hinds, "Record ID: WILT-71DA46 - POST MEDIEVAL Stopper."
20 Hinds, "Record ID: WILT-F46577 - MEDIEVAL Stopper."

For an Old Man that Travelled up and down the Country, and had some acquaintance at that house, calling in and asking the Man of the house how he did and his Wife; He told him that himself was well, but his Wife had been a long time in a languishing condition, and that she was haunted with a thing in the shape of a Bird, that would flurr [flutter] near to her face, and that she could not enjoy her natural rest well. The Old Man bid him and his Wife be of good courage. It was but a dead Spright, he said, and he would put him in a course to rid his Wife of this languishment and trouble. He therefore advised him to take a Bottle, and put his Wives Urine into it, together with Pins and Needles and Nails, and Cork them up, and set the Bottle to the fire, but be sure the Cork be fast in it, that it fly not out. The Man followed the prescription, and set the Bottle to the fire well corkt, which when it had felt a while the heat of the fire began to move and joggle a little, but he for sureness took the Fireshovel off, which he still quickly put on again, but at last at one shoving the Cork bounced out, and the Urine, Pins, Nails and needles all flew up, and gave a report like a Pistol, and his Wife continued in the same trouble and languishment still.

Not long after, the Old Man came to the house again, and inquired of the Man of the house how his Wife did. Who answered as ill as ever, if not worse. He askt him if he had followed his direction. Yes, says he, and told him the event as is abovesaid. Ha, quoth he, it seems it was too nimble for you. But now I will put you in a way, that will make the business sure. Take your Wive's Urine as before, and Cork it in a Bottle with Nails, Pins and Needles, and bury it in the Earth; and that will do the feat. The Man did accordingly. And his Wife began to mend sensibly, and in a competent time was finely well recovered. But there came a Woman from a Town some miles off to their house, with a lamentable Out-cry, that they had killed her Husband. They askt her what she meant and thought her distracted, telling her they knew neither her nor her husband. Yes, saith she, you have killed my husband, he told me so on his Death-bed. But at last they understood by her, that her Husband was a

> *Wizzard, and had bewitched this Mans Wife, and that this Counter-practice, prescribed by the Old Man, which saved the Mans Wife from languishment, was the death of that Wizzard that had bewitcht her.* [21]

Glanvil's account is not only quite detailed, it also presents both boiling and burying of witch bottles occurring in the same situation.

William Drage's *Daimonomageia* (1665) presents the following remedies for dealing with a witch:

> *Punish the thing bewitched; putting red hot Iron in the Churrn, when Butter would not come, hath burned her in the Guts; burning the Excrements of one bewitched, hath made her Anus sore; tying the Fat or Cauldron of Drink hard with Cords, that hath boiled over when scarce any Fire was under, hath made the Witch be sore girt and pained; stopping up Bottles of that Drink that hath been bewitched, hath made the Witch able neither to urine or deject, until they were opened...* [22]

Through the archaeological record, we have many examples of witch bottles made out of stoneware jugs with round bodies and thin necks, the latter of which was often decorated with a bearded man's face. Such jugs, usually used to transport beer, have since been dubbed "bellarmines," in mockery of the unpopular Catholic theologian Robert Bellarmine (1542-1621). These jugs were thought at one time to be similar to the face of Bellarmine, or even modelled after it. Today, this hypothesis is usually rejected, and terms such as "greybeard" and "Bartmann" are more accepted.[23] The earliest examples came from Cologne

---

21 Glanvil, *Saducismus Triumphatus*, 205–7. For more background on Brearly, see Merrifield, "Witch Bottles and Magical Jugs," 198–9.
22 Drage, *Daimonomageia*, 21. A similar charm appears in a fifteenth-century Dutch magical miscellany, aimed at harming someone who has stolen milk or beer. Braekman, *Magische Experimenten*, 11.
23 Orser, "Rethinking 'Bellarmine' Contexts in 17th-Century England.," 89.

and the Rhine Valley; the Netherlands and England itself were turning out similar vessels by the mid-seventeenth century.[24]

Bellarmines were likely in circulation in England for seventy years before they began to be used as witch bottles. It might be that the faces appearing on the bellarmines inspired their usage for anti-witchcraft spells. Still, the need for a bellarmine is not mentioned in the recipes or other accounts that have come down to us, raising the question as to how necessary they might have been to the procedure. It could be that the bellarmines were used because they were a ubiquitous container appropriate to the purpose. Other vessels might have also been used, with different rates of survival.[25] Another possibility might be that the witch bottle had its roots in the Rhine Valley, where so many bellarmines were produced.[26] Also, the switch from animal hearts to cloth hearts might have occurred to facilitate their placement in a bottle.

Bellarmine Bottle

---

24 Holmes, "The So-Called 'Bellarmine' Mask on Imported Rhenish Stoneware"; Haselgrove, "Imported Pottery in the 'Book of Rates," 326.
25 Merrifield, "The Use of Bellarmines as Witch-Bottles." One possible example, a green glass bottle, turned up in a chimney in Holburn though any contents were absent. Sumnall, "Record ID: LON-B416A6 - POST MEDIEVAL Bottle."
26 Thwaite, "Magic and the Material Culture of Healing," 212.

No matter their source, numerous bellarmine witch bottles have been found dating from the late seventeenth century. Several examples have been found in London, usually buried or tossed into the Thames. Even more have been found in East Anglia, particularly in Suffolk, although these usually have turned up the threshold or hearth of buildings from the period. In either case, these usually contain pins, with less common additions being a felt heart, hair, thorns, and nail clippings.[27] A particularly striking example from Suffolk includes the usual ingredients, along with shards of glass, brass studs, a fork, and spills (wooden pieces used to make matches).[28]

Further Examples of Bellarmines

The practice of creating such bottles travelled as far as Dublin, where a bellarmine dug up at a construction site was found with iron nails inside.[29]

---

27 Merrifield, "The Use of Bellarmines as Witch-Bottles"; Merrifield, *The Archaeology of Ritual and Magic*, 163–9; Peacock, "The Folklore of Lincolnshire." 176; Tilley, "A Witch-bottle from Gravesend."; Powell, "The Holywell Witch Bottle."
28 Merrifield and Smedley, "Two Witch-bottles from Suffolk."
29 Mulvihill, "Dublin's Weird 'Witch' Bottle." Not much information is available

Until recently, limitations on preservation and funding prevented any formal analysis of the contents of these witch bottles. In 2009, laboratories at Liverpool University, Leicester Royal Infirmary, and the British Geological Survey examined material inside a bellarmine found buried and inverted in Greenwich in 2004, with a later study appearing from Alan Massey of Loughborough University. The contents included urine (with trace amounts of cotinine, indicating a smoker), brass pins, fingernails, hair, iron needles (bent into hook shapes), sulfur, lint, and a possibly heart-shaped piece of leather.[30]

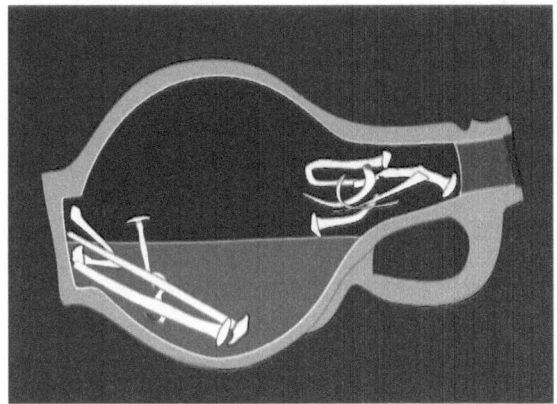

Drawing of an X-Ray showing the content of the Greenwich Bottle

The late seventeenth century also saw the first publication of the witch bottle procedure intended as a recipe. Joseph Blagrave, a gentleman and astrologer of Reading, Berkshire, published the following description of such a bottle in the *Astrological Practice of Physick* in 1671. This is preceded with an adaptation of the charm involving a pan:

> *Another way is to get two new horseshoes, heat one of them red hot, and quench him in the patients urine, then*

---

on this particular bottle at this time.
30 Pitts, "Urine to Navel Fluff"; Hoggard, *Magical House Protection*.

> *immediately nail him on the inside of the threshold of the door with three nails, the heel being upwards: then having the patients urine set it over the fire, and set a trivet over it, put into it three horse nails, and a little white salt: Then heat the other horshooe red hot, and quench him several times in the urine, and so let it boil and waste until all be consumed; do this three times and let it be near the change, full, or quarters of the Moon; or let the Moon be in Square or Opposition unto the Witches Significator*

Immediately following this is the commonly-cited witch bottle charm:

> *Another way is to stop the urine of the Patient, close up in a bottle, and put into it three nails, pins, or needles, with a little white Salt, keeping the urine alwayes warm: If you let it remain long in the bottle, it will endanger the witches life: for I have found by experience, that they will be grievously tormented making their water with great difficulty, if any at all, and the more if the Moon be in Scorpio in Square or Opposition to his Significator, when its done.*[31]

Blagrave also notes similar ceremonies that might be performed using the patient's blood or thatch from their house. He notes that the blood is considered more vital, and charms involving it are more effective. Boiling blood and urine is effective, he claims, because 'such is the subtlety of the Devil, that he will not suffer the Witch to infuse any poysonous matter into the body of man or beast, without some of the Witches blood mingled with it.' The afflicted witch must either bear the torment – as some are capable – or arrive at the place where the substance is heated to smell it and thereby gain release. Through allowing this link, Satan prepares his witches for their horrible ends, knowing that such a charm may lead them to great pain that foreshadows the torments of hell.[32]

---

31 Blagrave, *Blagraves Astrological Practice of Physick*, 154.
32 Ibid., 155.

Blagrave's text provided wide dissemination for the charm. When St. Merryn resident Thomasine Leverton was undergoing a difficult pregnancy, she consulted a cunning person. In September 1701, that individual wrote out a description of a procedure very close to Blagrave's model, that her client might overcome the ill wishes of her enemies.[33] The charm is as follows:

> *For Thomson Leverton on Saturday next, being the 17th of this instant September any time that day take about a pint of your own urine and make it almost scalding hot, then empty it into a stone jug with a narrow mouth, then put into it so much white salt as you can take up with the thumb and two forefingers of your left hand, and three new nails with their points downward, their points being first made very sharp. Then stop the mouth of the jug very close with a piece of tough clay and bind a piece of leather firm over the stop, then put the jug into warm embers and keep him there nine or ten days and nights following, so that it go not stark cold all that meantime, day nor night, and your private enemies will never after have any power upon you, either in body or goods. So be it.*[34]

This compares favourably with the previous rite, especially regarding the usage of salt and three sharp nails.

Another seventeenth-century witch bottle formula can be found in a collection of anti-witchcraft techniques in British Library Sloane 3846. This procedure is attributed to Roger Bacon, who is the son of the likely-mythical wizard and friar William Bacon, and may be used to address the bewitchment of men, women, children, cattle, bread, butter – a great range of misfortunes of the family farm.

---

33 Semmens, "The Usage of Witch-bottles and Apotropaic Charms in Cornwall," 26.
34 Thanks to Kresen Kernow for allowing me to publish X268/83 from their collection.

For this particular formula, a person's urine must be bottled with oil of populeon, a substance in which black poplar is the primary ingredient. This should be set on the fire, in the planetary hours attributed to Mars or Saturn, until it is about to boil over. Then the magician heats tongs to red hot and places them within, saying:

> *I conjure thee [A], witch or witches or wicked spirit, by the living God, the true God, and the holy God, and by the birth of Jesus Christ, his godly doctrine and wonders worked that he did upon the earth, and by his burial, resurrection, and ascension, and by all powers that are created and contained under the throne of God, and by all the powers propounded by me, I command and conjure thee [A], or you witches or wicked spirits, by all other powers that you are subject to, that you presently do depart from this N. in peace and unity and never to vex or trouble him or her any more, by any kind of diabolical powers earthly or ghostly, upon pain of everlasting condemnation, and for thy wicked deeds to be tormented with the fiery darts of hell, signed with a mark upon thy body or bodies, whereby thou mayest repent and be mended thy evil life. Fiat, fiat, fiat. Amen.*[35]

As with other bottles being created, it was possible that the witch would visit the magician to ask for an item. The manuscript tells the creator of the bottle to send this person away, saying,

> *Depart from my house and from my ground, thou wicked person, in the name of the Father, of the Son, and Holy Ghost. The cross of Jesus between thee and me from this time forth for evermore.*[36]

Using such a bottle was not necessarily safe, according to the tale of one woman tormented by evil spirits for three years. A relative seems to have placed the "Evil Spirit" "into a Stone Bottle that hung over the Fire" – most likely a witch bottle

---

35 British Library Sloane 3846, 96r.
36 Ibid.

procedure. He was surprised when he heard a roaring noise, followed by a loud bang and the room filling with smoke. Next, he was knocked down by an invisible force. The bottle shot up the chimney and was dropped back down, exuding smoke yet somehow unbroken. The woman was finally cured.[37]

Other experimenters, such as those whose activities are described in a ballad published in 1670, are reported to have had less perilous results. An unnamed girl living near the Blue Boar Inn, Holburn, was deeply harmed by witchcraft, and her friends despaired of her life. They sought out a "Chymist," or practitioner of Paracelsian magic:

> *This Girls own Urine then he bid them take,*
> *And with some other things a mixture make:*
> *Which being put into a bottle then,*
> *He ordered them the manner, place, and when.*
>
> *They should this Bottle in in [sic] a Dung hill put,*
> *Which he believ'd the witches Charms would cut*
> *This thing they then were all resolv'd to try,*
> *Hoping to find some help immediately.*

After they did so, the accused witch appeared and asked for the bottle. She was denied it, and later grew sick and died, with the girl making a full recovery.[38]

One account of witch bottles turns up in a record of the Norfolk assizes from Lent, 1671, describing an event in the 1650s in which a Great Yarmouth man believed himself to be bewitched. An unknown person suggested that he combine old "nails, pins, and needles" with a red cloth heart and an unspecified liquid in a bottle, placed over the fire. It seemed to cause discomfort to the suspected witch.[39]

---

37 Anonymous, *Strange and Wonderful Nevvs*, 5–7.
38 Anonymous, *A Miraculous Cure for VVitchcraft*.
39 National Archives at Kew, ASSI 16/21/3, quoted in Gaskill, "The Fear and Loathing of Witches," 131.

Witch bottles featured prominently in two witch trials in 1682. In March, Southwark resident Joan Buts was accused of striking Mary Farmer ill. Dr. Bourn, apparently a local cunning man, advised the girl's parents to stop up her urine in a bottle and bury it while burning her clothes to compel the witch to appear. Ms. Buts appeared with a hideous expression on her face and fell to writhing on the ground, making horrible sounds. Sadly, the charm seems to have been ineffective, as Mary soon passed away. [40]

In June, a similar case appeared at the court of Oyer and Terminer in London, with Jane Kent being accused of killing five-year-old Elizabeth Chamblet. When her mother was also attacked, her father sought the advice of a Doctor Hainks of Spitalfields. Under the doctor's instructions, the elder Chamblet boiled a pipkin containing a quart of Elizabeth's urine, hair, nail parings, and other items. He claimed he could hear the witch screaming outside the house, although he refused to open the door to see if she were there, and the next day she appeared swollen. Both Joan Buts and Jane Kent were acquitted at trial.[41]

Not all witch bottle usage became the subject of trials. Author and antiquary John Aubrey relates how a local man owned a horse that became uncontrollable due to witchcraft. He buried a bottle of urine from the horse, and the man believed to be responsible eventually died of an inability to urinate. When dug up, the bottle was mostly empty; locals believed that a witch who survived until the vessel was empty could regain his or her health.[42]

This was not the only case in which a witch bottle was created for a horse, as Thomas Tryon indicated:

---

40 Anonymous, *An Account of the Tryal and Examination of Joan Buts*, 3–4.
41 Great Britain Court of Oyer and Terminer and Gaol Delivery (London and Middlesex), *A Full and True Account...*, 3–4; Anonymous, *True Narrative of the Proceedings*, 3.
42 Aubrey, *Miscellanies ...*, 112.

> *'Tis said, That a Horse being Bewitched, they filled a Bottle with the Horses Urine, stop'd it well with a Cork, and bound it fast in, and then Buried it under Ground, and the party fell ill that was suspected to be the Witch, and could not make Water, of which she died.*[43]

Our final witch bottle from this period, in a bellarmine made in the last two decades of the seventeenth century, was found in a hearth at Hellington, Norfolk, in 1976. In addition to eight hawthorn thorns and a string with three reef knots, it also contained fragments of a printed French prayer book, part of which was tied up in hair and pierced with a brass pin. The text remains indecipherable.[44]

Whatever their history before, witch bottles had become popular and accepted in many parts of England. Further, although we know little about the identities of those who recommended such procedures, it seems that a wide range of people, ranging from practitioners of Paracelsian magic to cunning folk to those with little medical knowledge, believed the experiment to be useful in alleviating illness.[45]

THE EIGHTEENTH CENTURY

The beginning of the eighteenth century saw no cessation in the use of witch bottles. One controversial account from Northampton tells of two women, Mary Phillips and Elinor Shaw, being accused of attacking twelve-year-old Charles Ireland in 1705. His mother buried a bottle of pins, needles, and his urine in the hearth, causing both suspects to come to the house and promise to free the boy of their enchantments.[46] On February 17, 1712, servant girl Anne Thorn was exceedingly ill,

---

43 Tryon, *The Way to Save Wealth*, 50.
44 Walker, "A Witch Bottle from Hellington."
45 Thwaite, "What Is a 'Witch Bottle'?," 242–48.
46 Davis, "An Account of the Tryals, Examination and Condemnation, of Elinor Shaw, and Mary Phillip's," 4–5.

supposedly due to one Jane Wenham's enchantment. On that evening, others placed a bottle of Anne's urine over the fire and sent observers to the supposed witch's house. Wenham was afflicted with crying and horrible pain until the cork flew out of the bottle with a loud noise.[47]

Wenham was sentenced to death, but later pardoned. This turned out to be the last conviction under the 1604 Witchcraft Act, and an impetus for the passage of another in 1736. The new law officially transformed the government's views of the dangers of witchcraft from murder and destruction to fraud and fortune-telling. This did little to dissuade most people from believing in witchcraft, or seeking magical solutions thereto.[48] Indeed, the lack of official recourse would have made believers turn to witch bottles and other remedies.

In 1717, a group of women at Leicester believed themselves to be tormented by witches. To fight them off, they followed a cunning man's advice to place a bewitched person's urine in a bottle by the fire. Their account is notable for their experimentation with the procedure, and the circumstances surrounding it:

> ...which they frequently did and cork^d it well and ty'd down the cork wth 20 rounds of packthread, notwithstanding which the water w^t. allways give a crack like a gun, & the cork fly out leaving the bottle and pack thread as it was, while the water was in the bottle the afflicted parties had ease but upon its bursting out their pains & illness return'd.
>
> The good women who gave information depos'd, that for experiment sake they used to stew their own water so, but their's would never crack or fiz or fly away like the other, but would symmer as quietly when it was heated as any spring water.

---

47 Bragge, A Full and Impartial Account of the Discovery of Sorcery and Witchcraft, 20.
48 Davies, "Decriminalising the Witch."

> *When the patients urine was set to stew by the fire some one of the witches was allways observed to come into the room sometimes in the shape of a cat & sometimes a dog… these dogs and cats would come in tho: the doors and windows were shut and all passages except keyholes & chimneys stopt & could never be catch^d but would grin furiously, and approaching near the bewitch'd persons give them great pain and so vanish.*[49]

In 1762, the two daughters of Richard Giles at Lawford's Gate, Bristol became the victims of mysterious spiritual assaults; stabbings with pins and spectral fingernails, poltergeist activity intense enough to move heavy wagons, an apparition of an old woman, and a presence that scratched out responses to requests made in English, Latin, and Greek. The situation became dire enough that Mr. Giles himself died of fever, believed to have been due to the stress under which the spirit placed him. In the end, his widow petitioned a cunning woman at Bedminster, who told her to place her children's urine in a pipkin over a fire. If she saw colours like a rainbow in the liquid as it boiled, the girls could be cured. The widow did so, and the manifestations stopped.[50]

A manuscript from the collection of the antiquary Francis Douce, now at the Bodleian Library, includes an item copied from the *Morning Post* from May 29, 1792, the printed version of which does not seem to have survived. An Uxbridge farmer was having trouble with one horse, then another, of a mysterious nature. Placing a bottle with horse urine and crooked pins into the fire, the farmer watched it explode, and the horses recovered.[51]

---

49 Ewen, Great Britain Courts of Assize and Nisi Prius, *Witch Hunting and Witch Trials*, 314–5.
50 Durbin, *A Narrative of Some Extraordinary Things*. The account bears many striking resemblances to the supposed Bell Witch case of Tennessee, save for being more bizarre.
51 Douce 116, xvi. Printed edition in Harms and Aldarnay, *The Book of Four Wizards*.

As with the seventeenth century, the presence of buried witch bottles takes us beyond recorded records. One glass bottle, found in a grave in All Saints Church, Loughton, bore a cork studded with copper pins and is believed to date circa 1700.[52] Another, deposited after 1720 at Reigate, is one of the few that has been subjected to chemical analysis, albeit years after originally being opened. Nine bent and corroded bronze pins were found, along with high amounts of nitrate which may indicate the presence of urine. Other ingredients included plant matter, animal and human hairs, dyed cotton fibre, wool, linen, silica, and other substances. It is unclear as to whether these were deliberately included in the bottle when originally sealed.[53] At some point between 1700 and 1740, the inhabitants of one dwelling in Shoreditch filled a late seventeenth-century bellarmine with bent pins and placed it beneath their floors.[54]

On the north side of the churchyard of All Saints Church in Loughton, Buckinghamshire, archaeologists found a bottle with copper pins both inside and stuck into the cork, buried with the body of an individual around twenty years of age and of indeterminate sex. A parallel might be found below, with a witch bottle found buried in a Bodmin cemetery.[55]

Stockton-on-Tees provides us with a handsome example of a potential witch bottle, a green glass item with a long neck and silver stopper. It appears to have been placed in the cupola of the town hall during its construction around 1735, later being rediscovered during renovation in the 1840s. If so, it is an unusual case of a bottle being placed both at the top of a building, and in a municipal structure instead of a home or

---

52 Hoggard, "The Archaeology of Counter-Witchcraft and Popular Magic," 174.
53 Massey and Edmonds, "The Reigate Witch Bottle."
54 Lewis, "From Prehistoric to Urban Shoreditch," 253–54.
55 Buckinghamshire County Museum Archaeological Service, *Archaeological Investigations at All Saints Church, Loughton, Milton Keynes*, [4-5].

public house. The original contents of the bottle, now in the collection of the Preston Park Museum, are unknown.[56]

Another notable eighteenth-century example is a tiny bottle found near the chimney of a house in Debenham, Suffolk. The specimen was fitted with a modern cork when found in the Seventies, but it contained hair and most likely urine as well.[57] A mid-century bottle found beneath a parish boundary wall in Dorset included animal fat among its ingredients, possibly to ward off injuries to the parish cattle.[58] In an article on the dating of glass, Fowler reports on two glass phials found beneath churches in south Leicestershire. He believed that both were more recent in character, and that they may have been examples of witch bottles, due to their upside-down positioning.[59]

In addition to the St. Merryn recipe noted above, we have one other example of a witch bottle recipe from this century. Dating to about 1730, it appears in a set of documents auctioned in 2020 by the Dominic Winter firm, which was good enough to post a facsimile on their website. The wife of a household should fast and put their water into a quart-sized stone bottle in the morning, along with a lock of hair from one's crown, two nails, and a finger (hopefully meaning the fingernail), along with nails and pins that should be crooked and rusty and some small bent pieces of iron. One should add personal items of one's husband and finally spit into the bottle just before corking it after he comes home. The couple should sit up all night, boiling the bottle in water, and then hang it in the chimney in the morning. Hanging St. John's wort about the house is also suggested as a helpful addition.[60]

---

56 White, "Witch Bottle with a Halloween Link Is Object of the Week."
57 King and Massey, "A Miniature Witch Bottle?".
58 Massey, Smith, and Smith, "A Witch Bottle from Dorset."
59 Fowler, "On the Process of Decay in Glass," 132–3.
60 Dominic Winter Auctioneers, "Lot 242."

THE NINETEENTH CENTURY

By the early nineteenth century, multiple generations of British citizens had never witnessed trials for witchcraft, yet the belief in the existence and impact of witches was still strong in many areas. The mid-century rise in professional policing ramped up prosecutions of the cunning folk who made witch bottles under the Witchcraft or Vagrancy Acts, yet it also worked against vigilante justice against suspected witches, potentially making the usage of counter-magic more popular.[61]

William Bottrell, the Cornish folklorist and raconteur, told a tale of a Cornish witch bottle rite from approximately 1800. Captain Matthew Thomas of Treen, near Zennor, loved panning for tin and smuggling with his crew. He let his estate run down until the fences broke and his cattle wandered into the fields of his neighbours. Soon his livestock became sick, and he sought out An Maggey, the cross-dressing, pistol-wielding white witch of Zennor, in her hut by the ocean. Maggey, after admonishing the captain for his lax attitude toward his property, corked a bottle of the sick animals' urine, and Thomas hid it in the pile of tin behind his house.

Gossips soon broadcast the operation throughout the parish. As unpopular as Captain Thomas was, dozens of locals felt themselves under the influence of the witch bottle, their psychosomatic pains enhanced by ongoing comparison with those of their fellows. One night, they decided to band together to attack the smugglers in the house of their tinworks, in the hope of relief. The smugglers saw them coming and discharged their firearms, driving them off. The fleeing Zennor residents ran into the parson of nearby Gulval, who was hunting with

---

61 Davies, *Witchcraft, Magic and Culture*; Waters, *Cursed Britain*, 9-37.

some gentlemen. He brokered a peace deal, and the captain broke open the bottle in front of the assemblage.[62]

The nineteenth century brought many technological innovations, with iron witch bottles among the most surprising. While promising relief from supernatural harm, they brought with them mundane dangers, as this account shows:

> *In the month of May 1804, a Bradford weaver, named Sutcliffe, began to imagine that his house was haunted by an evil spirit. Desirous of abating its mischievous influence he resorted to a notorious local wizard, who readily promised his assistance in doing so. Having poured a quantity of human blood mixed with hair into a large iron bottle, the designing knave corked it tightly and placed it on the fire where it soon exploded with a terrific report, killing the weaver on the spot.[63]*

In 1808, Isaac Nicholson, reverend of the parish of Great Paxton, found that one of his parishioners was a suspected victim of witchcraft. Her brother had heard a cure from a man in Bedfordshire, with an unusual take on the bottle as a divination device:

> *He filled a bottle with a particular kind of a fluid, stuffed the cork both top and bottom, with pins, set it carefully in an oven of a moderate heat, and then observed with a profound silence. In a few minutes the charm succeeded; for he saw a variety of forms flitting before his eyes, and amongst the rest the perfect resemblance of an old woman who lived in the same parish... he was now satisfied who it was that had injured him, and that her reign would soon be over.[64]*

---

62 Bottrell, *Traditions and Hearthside Stories of West Cornwall*, vol. 1. 83-6. Bottrell was known to embroider tales, as was the custom with a storyteller of his time.
63 Sydney, *The Early Days of the Nineteenth Century in England, 1800-1820*, vol. 2. 73.
64 Nicholson, *A Sermon against Witchcraft*, iii.

During his research on Somerset cunning folk and witchcraft beliefs, Owen Davies came across several notable cases involving witch bottles. A Wells cunning man gave one of his clients the following incantation to recite:

> *In the name of Christ I put these pins, thorns, & c. into this bottle, and I wish them not so much to be there as in the heart of the person that has done me this mischief.*

In this instance, a vial of urine was to be filled with seven each of white thorns, black thorns, pins, and headless nails, to be stoppered and hidden beneath the hearth at a quarter to twelve – whether before noon or midnight is not stated.[65] If an anti-witchcraft ritual observed in East Anglia is any indication, midnight seems more likely:

> *...the most effectual remedy, or mode of exorcism, is to take a quantity of the patient's urine, and boil it with nine nails from as many old horseshoes. The process is to begin exactly at midnight. The conductress of it is to have an assistant to obey orders, but is to touch nothing herself... A single word mars the whole charm. At a certain critical point in the process, when three, five, or seven of the nails have been put in motion at once... (for some cases are more difficult than others), the spirit is cast out...*[66]

The author goes on to describe an assistant who spoke upon seeing the spirit escaping, with dire consequences to the patient.

One of the most well-known nineteenth-century advocates of the witch bottle was James 'Cunning' Murrell (1785-1860) of Hadleigh, Essex. Arthur Morrison, writing a profile for *The Strand* nearly fifty years later, mentioned Murrell's use of

> *the iron witch-bottles made for Murrell by Choppen the smith, in which were placed blood, water, finger-nails, hair, and pins; which bottles, when screwed up air-tight, were set on the fire by way of process against witches, and frequently burst*

---

65 Davies, *A People Bewitched*.
66 Forby, *The Vocabulary of East Anglia*, vol. 2. 394.

> *with great success and devastation, thus signalizing the destruction of the diabolical influence.*[67]

Choppen's first efforts at creating such a bottle apparently met with failure, until Murrell said a charm over the forge. The smith is believed to have left a small hole in one end of the bottles, to lower the risk of detonation. Local legend has it that a boy, kept in the dark as to the bottle's purpose, was convinced to drink beer out of it, dying of fear after being told what it was.[68] Even after this supposed tragedy, these creations were used to great effect, according to a Mrs. Watson, when a local girl was driven mad after turning out a Romany woman from her barn:

> *Murrell was called in. He placed in the fire a bottle containing hair and nail-clippings from the victim. He told everyone to keep absolutely silent while they awaited the arrival of the witch. Presently there came a hammering on the door, and a woman's voice begged him to stop 'the test,' as the fire was causing her agony. The bottle burst. On the following morning, an old woman was found burned to death outside the Woodcutters' Arms, three miles away. It was the gypsy. The girl recovered.*[69]

These did not always have successful results for the patient, as an 1849 story in *Lloyd's Weekly Newspaper* relates. Although Murrell is not named in the story, it occurs within a few miles of his home. The iron bottle blew up and destroyed the grate to which it had been padlocked.[70]

Ironically, another charmer from Rayleigh would claim that Murrell's death was due to his own use of a witch bottle. According to his story, upon finding that a donkey was ill, the Rayleigh cunning man placed both his nail parings and the donkey's hair inside a bottle. He placed it on the fire and

---

67 Morrison and Maple, *Marsh Wizards, Witches and Cunning Men*, 11.
68 Maple, *The Dark World of Witches*, 168.
69 Ibid., 43–44.
70 "Provincial Intelligence."

ignored the insistent knocking at his door until it burst. The following day, he learned that Murrell had passed.[71]

Murrell's practice passed to his son Buck, who decided to keep up his reputation by using one of the surviving containers. Unfortunately, his client disregarded his instruction to remain silent, and the bottle exploded, taking out a substantial part of the chimney and nearly one side of his house with it[72].

Nineteenth-century witch bottles need not have been iron, and were employed in the city as well as the country. William Dawson Bellhouse (1814-1870) was a galvanist and cunning man living in Leeds and Liverpool, with a clientele eager to experience electricity, astrology, and charms. His own magical notebook, dated 1852, includes a rite with an impressive list of ingredients:

To hurt or destroy a witch

Cut a little hair of the nap[e] of the neck of the afflicted person or party bewitched and with parings of finger and toe nails and some of his blood, and three quarts of his water a chain of seven links, the middle link to turn down, and the heart of a fowl fresh, and three new needles, and three new pins. Take them and stick them in the heart a few rusty nails and cards teeth[73]. Then take three pennyworth of aqua fortis, th[r]ee pennyworth of vitriol, three pennyworth of french flies [cantharides], three pennyworth of brims[t]on[e], three pennyworth of devil's dung [asafoetida], 3c pennyworth of dragon's blood, and in smaller bottles, put three drams of each. Those most be all put in a strong bottle that withstand[s] fire, or a pan, and boil them on a slow fire until all is consumed. The chain must be half red hot before it is put in. Stir it with a red hot poker five or six times, and say, turning the poker, these words: 'Witch, witch, witch, I thee burn (or I thee kill) in hellfire if thou does not leave this person, and evil turn to thyself, thou shall feel the wrath of

---

71 Adshead, "Canewdon and Its Witches."
72 Morrison and Maple, *Marsh Wizards, Witches and Cunning Men*, 15–17.
73 These refer to the teeth on a wool card or comb.

*God for evermore. Amen." After this read the 70ᵗʰ Psalm. If a pan is used, scrape all well out, and bring it at the north side of the house, and this will finish it.*⁷⁴

This charm has some fascinating aspects. It is versatile enough to be used with a pan or a bottle, and in fact the appearance of both possibilities suggests that the one evolved into another. Further, it incorporates the heated chain, which draws parallels with anti-witchcraft rites to scald a witch by inserting a hot object into milk. Some of the ingredients are not found elsewhere – were these Bellhouse's innovations?

Later in the same work, Bellhouse offers a simpler version, which seems to be an elaboration on Blagrave's formula:

To Kill a Witch

*Take a new stone bottle, and put into it two quarts of the person's water that be afflicted. Get three new needles and crooked pins. Get the heart of the fowl, and stick the needles and pins in the heart, also the parings of all the fingers and toe nails, and a little hair from the neck hole, and a little of his blood, some salt and soot. Boil all over a slow fire, stopped or corked up, until all is consumed.*⁷⁵

A variety of mid-nineteenth century bottles have also been discovered. Perhaps the most elaborate came out of Ram Mark Pond near Yeovil in 1854. Inside a pickle jar was a piece of lead carved with magical symbols and three figurines, partially made of gutta-percha latex, filled with black pins. The front of each bore the astrological symbol of Saturn, while the backs were inscribed with the names of two local constables and one of their wives, along with the statement that they would undergo "sudden destruction, legal and moral." One of the constables had been ill, but he recovered after the bottle was found. The perpetrator was never caught.⁷⁶

---

74 Bellhouse, "A Complete System of Magic." 28-29.
75 Bellhouse, "A Complete System of Magic." 29
76 Davies, *A People Bewitched*.

A curious yellow stone bottle of indeterminate date was found in a Wharfedale farmer's garden in 1845. The contents included human hair, brimstone, needles, pins, and fingernail clippings. No liquid contents are described.[77]

During roadworks at Holywood, Stockport, workers found two bottles of purplish fluid buried six inches deep beneath long grass. Analysis found that the contents were dragon's blood, urine, and pins. When reporters asked around the area, they found that such practices were commonly known in the area. One practitioner claimed that dumping these items in the cesspool or garden would lead to the destruction of nearby crops. Only by breaking the bottle over running water and casting the pieces in afterward would break the spell.[78]

One prominent witch bottle in the news was found in a chimney of the former Star and Garter Inn in Watford, Northamptonshire. The bottle, of a type used since the 1830s to contain carbonated soda, included an unspecified liquid, fishhooks, and human teeth. In 1761, Angeline Tubbs was born at the inn; she later emigrated to New York state and became known as the "Witch of Saratoga." Of course, she had left England well before the witch bottle's creation. The current owner seems to have returned the bottle to another hiding place in the structure.[79]

Drawing based on the bottle from the Star and Garter Inn, Watford

---

77 Bogg, *Lower Wharfeland*, 346.
78 "Witchcraft in Stockport."
79 British Broadcasting Corporation, "Ancient Anti-Witchcraft Potion Found at Old Northamptonshire Pub."

The Bottesford author and antiquarian Edward Peacock found several witch bottles, reporting on the first two in 1856. One was buried in proximity to an ox or horse in a man's garden in Yaddlethorpe, while another close to his hometown contained the heart of a small animal.[80] This was not Peacock's only discovery; by 1880, his demolishing cottages on his estates had turned up at least a dozen such objects beneath the buildings' foundations.[81] He also noted that witchcraft could be countered if one buried a bottle containing urine, pins, and hair under the eaves.[82]

A doll's head accompanied a witch bottle was discovered recently in a wooded area near Oswestry, Shropshire. The bottle itself, dated between 1860 and the end of the century, was sealed with wax and cork, and contained liquid, hair and a tooth. It is unclear whether the doll head and the witch bottle were buried at the same time. Chris Langston, the metal detectorist who found the bottle, returned it to the ground nearby.[83]

The latter part of the century also features several accounts of witch bottle usage, often related by clients of the cunning folk who instructed them in their use. The first was a woman who consulted a cunning woman near Guildford regarding her daughter's epilepsy. The remedy was to fill a quart bottle with pins, which were then placed on the fireplace until the pins "would prick the heart of the witch" who had laid the charm. The second describes a bottle hidden under the hearthstone of a Pulborough house during renovations. Unfortunately, the ritual to create it was dismissed by the teller as "ludicrous, but unfit for him to relate"[84].

---

80 Peacock, "Replies: Easter Sunday Superstitions."
81 Fowler, "On the Process of Decay in Glass," 133.
82 Peacock, *A Glossary of Words Used in the Wapentakes of Manley and Corringham, Lincolnshire*, 193.
83 Wheeler and Coussins, "Man Spooked."
84 Latham, "Some West Sussex Superstitions Lingering in 1868," 25–26.

In 1855, a man in Langford believed that his landlord's wife was responsible for a chronic illness for which doctors could find no cause. He spoke with a local wise man, who performed a ritual for the price of a sovereign. Beginning with a "game of cards" – it's not clear whether this was part of the ritual or not – several bottles of pins and "stuff" were placed in the fire. Following this, the cunning man recited the 37th Psalm three times in reverse. A bottle with a "heart" filled with pins, along with "stuff," was capped with a pin-filled cork and buried under the floor. The landlord's wife fell victim to a mysterious illness, as if being pricked with pins, and the condition only lifted once the bottle was removed.[85]

One J. B., a farmer in Hockham, Norfolk, believed his wife had been bewitched. A cunning woman advised them to combine horseshoe nails, nail parings, hair from the wife's neck, and "some particular liquid" in a bottle. When the bottle was placed in the fire and exploded, the witch would appear – apparently not so dangerous a charm to the witch as others, it seems. The woman appeared, and the farmer asked the local magistrate if she might be cast into water to see if she would float. The magistrate declined to "swim the witch," to the farmer's disappointment.[86]

Frederick Culliford of Crewkerne was put on trial in 1876 for obtaining money under false pretenses. At the local market he met Emma Foot, who sought a remedy for her sick mother. Culliford recommended that she place thorns and a piece of paper in a bottle of the mother's urine, to be buried in the garden. She did so, later digging it up and breaking it when her mother's condition did not improve. The paper held a surprising statement:

---

85 "Superstition in Langport."
86 E., "Witchcraft in the Present Day: To the Editor of the Times."

> *As long as this paper remains in this bottle of water of mine I hope that Satan, that angel of darkness, will pour out his wrath upon the person that has been privately injuring of me... and as this water is fomented and troubled with these thorn prickles so shall the flesh on their body be also fomented... and they shall not live for more than 90 days from this day and no longer, and then go to hell everlasting...*

Culliford was placed in jail for a year, and Emma's mother eventually improved.[87]

That same year, a concerned shopkeeper on High-Street, Barnstaple, wrote the *North Devon Journal* to report an odd occurrence. A customer asked for a new cork and bottle – specifically, one that had never had water inside. She was going to fill it with needles and pins and stopper it, after which the witch afflicting her would feel the steel points in her heart and come to her. This remedy had already worked for her once before.[88]

The following decade, witch bottles became part of love spells. In 1888, Adelina Westernoff appeared before the mayor in Chesterfield to answer a charge of fraud. Another local woman, Deborah Wood, had had a child before she was married, but the father was gone, and Wood wanted more money. Westernoff advised her to write her name on a heart-shaped piece of paper, which was inserted, along with three pins of different lengths and a mysterious powder, into a bottle. After this bottle was carefully corked and tied with string, to prevent explosion, Wood was to keep it in her bosom for nine days, at the end of which the man would reappear. The mayor sentenced Westernoff to two months of hard labour.[89]

Another witch bottle for love turned up in Brierley in 1894. Lilian Haynes was upset when her boyfriend took up with

---

87 Davies, *A People Bewitched*.
88 P., "Witchcraft in North Devon."
89 "'Witchcraft' at Chesterfield."

another woman in the same house. She appealed to two women, Mary Ann Smith and Mary Jane Pritchard, who charged her for a solution. They provided her with a bottle containing red liquid, and she dropped pins into it while reciting, "I wish that Ted Highway would depart from Louisa Jones and return to me, Lilly Haynes; may he not rest, asleep or awake, until he has done so." She was to continue inserting pins and making wishes; by the time the case reached the magistrates, the bottle contained thirteen pins. The two women were fined; Ted and Louisa remained happily together.[90]

In 1895, a jar of contemporary manufacture, with several pin and thorns within, was found in the churchyard of Bradworthy, North Devon. The discoverer was told that such a charm should be buried in three different churchyards to be effective.[91] Another Devonshire charm from that period is as follows: "To free oneself from a witch, bury three stoneware jars, each bearing a toad's heart transfixed with thorns and a frog's liver filled with pins, under different paths in a churchyard, while reciting the Lord's Prayer backwards".[92] Another bottle, buried bottom up and filled with nine bent pins and what appeared to be dark water, appeared when a farmhouse floor in Leekfrith, Staffordshire was excavated.[93]

The witch bottle practice expanded in this time to three geographic areas in which it had rarely been seen before. The first of these was Scotland. The demolition of a cottage in north Scotland in 1858 turned up five or six examples of witch bottles, including ones containing needles and human hair.[94] Campbell provides an example from turn of the century Scotland, to be used when a cow does not give milk. Boiling the animal's urine

---

90 "'Bewitching' a Young Man," 3.
91 Wellacott, "A Churchyard Charm."
92 Hewett, *Nummits and Crummits*, 74.
93 Beresford, "Notes on a Portion of the Northern Borders of Staffordshire," 101.
94 Longman and Loch, *Pins and Pincushions*, 38.

in a bottle prevents the witch from excreting until the witch is released. A similar procedure involves inserting pins into the creature's dung or milk, then boiling them until the cow is free of enchantment.[95]

A lengthier account comes from New Deer in Aberdeenshire. A local witch cursed a neighbour's cow, and it ceased to yield milk. A cunning woman suggested that a fire be lit on a hill, the cow led around it widdershins three times, and its urine corked up in a bottle which would be watched during the night. The witch showed up at the appointed hour, complaining of dreams that compelled her to appear. Eventually she was given access and agreed to free the cow from the spell.[96] We still only have few examples from Scotland, so it is uncertain how common the practice might have been there.

Second, although Glanvil's method of creating witch bottles was known in Wales from the early eighteenth century, the first known example from the country appears at this time. In 1871, while digging at Penrhos Bradwen farm in Holyhead, a labourer turned up a pot made in Buckley. Inside, pins pierced the remains of a frog, while a slate on top bore the name "Nanny Roberts." This seems to have been a common practice in the region at the time.[97]

The third locale, and the one in which it became most prominent, was Cornwall. Although we have the examples above of a formula from St. Merryn in 1701 and Bottrell's story from Zennor, it does not seem to have become a common procedure until this period. Around 1880, a hiker near Tintagel

---

[95] Campbell, *Witchcraft & Second Sight in the Highlands & Islands of Scotland*, 14. A similar charm involving milk has been recorded in a Nova Scotia fishing community. Rose, "Canadian Folklore," 125.
[96] Gregor, "Stories of Fairies from Scotland," 57–58.
[97] P., *Cas Gan Gythraul*, 115. Gruffydd, "Buckley Pot Used in Witchcraft." The National Museum of Wales claims an 18th century example was found at Allt-y-Rhiw Farm, near Llansilin, but the only mentioned content was lead. National Museum of Wales, "Witch-bottles and Healing Charms."

was told that an old stone cross – likely that at Bossiney – had fallen over, with several bottles with water and pins being found beneath. At Boscastle, he was informed that such items, if buried at wayside crosses, would reverse the ill wishes of others.[98] The discovery and destruction of several bottles filled with pins and water in 1892 led to a Camborne woman recovering from a lengthy illness. This might be seen as an inversion of the usual formula – or perhaps it reflects the woman's belief that she possessed powers that were turned against her.[99]

The Cornish folklorist Robert Hunt provides a case in which a local man buried a bottle of "waater" in order to free a piglet of a witch's spell.[100] He also records a Cornish charm in which a person touches each wart with a separate pin. The pins are placed in a bottle then buried at a crossroads or a new grave. One such bottle was placed in a grave at Bodmin, where the vicar found it.[101] Bottles buried beneath or placed inside houses have been found at Helston, Sennen, Tresmeer, and Padstow. One unusual bottle, found at Trevone near Padstow in the Thirties, includes several miniature Instruments of the Passion, including a cross, a ladder, axes, pincers, and stakes.[102]

THE TWENTIETH CENTURY

By the early twentieth century, the practices of the cunning folk, who had done so much to advocate the continued use of witch bottles, were falling into abeyance. Trains, automobiles, and publications brought Britain closer together, and both belief

---

98 Whitley, "Cornish Folklore"; Semmens, "The Usage of Witch-bottles and Apotropaic Charms in Cornwall," 27, 28
99 Semmens, "The Usage of Witch-Bottles and Apotropaic Charms in Cornwall," 28.
100 Hunt, *Popular Romances of the West of England*, 319.
101 Hunt, *Popular Romances of the West of England*, Ser. 2, 210.
102 Semmens, "The Usage of Witch-bottles and Apotropaic Charms in Cornwall," 28; Merrifield, "Witch Bottles and Magical Jugs," 196–97.

in witches and the small-farm agriculture, in which they played an important role, had fallen into abeyance. Thus, we only find a few examples of witch bottles that seem to arise from traditional practice.

A sexton at Monkleigh Parish in Devon turned up a mysterious bottle in 1900 filled with dark liquid and several pins inserted into the cork at the top. After it attracted the attention of some passers-by, the sexton reburied it. The vicar of the parish believed it was of recent vintage.[103] Three years later, a barbershop patron in Bishops Stortford, Essex, asked the barber for hair from the nape of his neck. It was to be placed in a bottle with nail clippings and water on the fire at midnight to revenge a wrong done to him.[104] A similar tradition could be found at Horseheath, Cambridgeshire. A bottle containing hair from the nape of the neck, water, shoe nails, nail parings, and pins, should be placed in a fire at midnight in complete silence.[105]

St. Augustine's Church in Wembley was built in 1908 and demolished in 1973. Beneath a concrete floor, a glass wine bottle was found, containing an unknown liquid and a small ceramic figurine of a hunched-over old woman with an arm missing. Its present whereabouts are unknown.[106]

According to one oral account, a farm in North Devon had seen a series of misfortunes around 1910. The locals called upon a "white witch" from Exeter, who recommended that "water" be placed into a jar near the chimney until someone showed up to ask for it. This led to animosity between the two families for decades.[107]

---

103 Amery, "A Witch's Bottle."
104 Kelway, *Memorials of Old Essex*, 251.
105 Parsons, "Notes on Cambridgeshire Witchcraft," 42–3.
106 Merrifield, *The Archaeology of Ritual and Magic*, 182.
107 Hoggard, *Magical House Protection*.

A Sussex woman in 1919 suspected a man of bewitching her garden. She often shut up the house and boiled pins in urine to bring him to her and, presumably, lift the curse, an act she had yet to bring about with her procedure.[108]

In one case, the bottle seems to have been employed to cast a curse rather than reverse one. A Dorset farmer in 1912, faced with ill health and a failing orchard, found a curious wax-sealed bottle, containing vipers and a centipede in spirits of wine, under one of his apple trees. Showing it to a local cunning woman, she advised him to bury it far away, break it, and cover it up, after which he had no trouble.[109]

The town of Canewdon in Essex has become famous for its witch lore, most notably that surrounding George Pickingill, the supposed "King of the Witches". When researching its folklore, Eric Maple learned that a witch whose charm had been reversed would acquire a circular brand on her face. One informant recalled a bottle being used in her childhood, with the witch scratching on the door of the house until someone spoke accidentally and neutralized the charm. A 'white witch' living in Canewdon, who had known Pickingill as a girl, still created witch bottles to help her clients.[110]

---

108 Anonymous, "Witchcraft in Sussex."
109 Rawlence, "Sundry Folk-lore Reminiscences Relating to Man and Beast in Dorset and the Neighbouring Counties," 59–60.
110 Morrison and Maple, *Marsh Wizards, Witches and Cunning Men*, 56–7; Howard, *East Anglian Witches and Wizards*, 115.

Witch Bottles in Scandinavia

Witch bottles are not necessarily a phenomenon exclusive to Britain and its colonies. In his article *"On the Process of Decay in Glass,"* James Fowler mentions that Professor George Stephens of Copenhagen had found many examples of such bottles from the seventeenth and eighteenth centuries in Denmark, buried in "out-of-the-way places." No further reports of bottles from that land and period have turned up, and I have yet to find any trace of either the letter Stephens sent to Fowler or the bottles themselves in Stephens' collection.[111] Nonetheless, the following examples, both from the nineteenth century, show that this practice had made its way from England to Scandinavia by that time.

In 1872, the court for the Danish hundreds of Bjerge and Aasum prosecuted Jørgen Larsen of Nørre Lyndelse parish for using charms for healing. One part of his rituals involved the creation of what would be an unambiguous witch bottle if found in England. First, his fingernails and toenails should be cut in an order – right hand, left foot, left, hand, right foot – as to create a cross shape. After that, the parings, the patient's hair, and a quantity of urine should be combined in a bottle, which is then buried in the churchyard in the most recent grave. Larsen was eventually acquitted because he had faith in his own charms and was not defrauding his customers[112].

We also have one written formula, collected in the Fron municipality of Gudbrandsdalen, Norway, circa 1830:

---

111 Fowler, "On the Process of Decay in Glass," 133.
112 Boberg, *Danske Folketro Samlet Af Jens Kamp*, 191–92; Henningsen, "Witchcraft Persecution after the Era of the Witch Trials," 146.

If a person has been fördjord[113], put his urine in a bottle with new, unused needles or pins, numbering 21, 24, or 51, all the same size. Cork it, bind a piece of hide or cloth over it, and put it in a secret place. On a Thursday eve, put a kettle on the stove and hang the bottle from a stick over it. The bottle may not touch the sides or the bottom of the kettle. Boil the water as violently as possible, keep all doors well-shut, and be still and silent. The person who did the evil will come and ask you to remove the kettle from the stove because it burns him, but you must not remove it until he has made the diseased person well again or given advice that you can use. When this is done, remove the kettle from the stove so he may be at ease and leave. Do as he instructed that evening or early next morning, when all is still and you are alone.[114]

It may be that further exploration of the literature and folklore of this region will yield us more examples.

---

113 *Fördjord*: Bewitched.
114 Original: Bang, *Norske Hexeformularer og magiske Opskrifter ...*, vol. I, 344–5. Translation: Gårdbäck, *Trolldom*, 266.

Witch Bottles in North America

EARLY EXAMPLES

Evidence for witch bottles in North America is sparser than that from England, and none of the traditional bellarmine witch bottles have been found in New World excavations. Nonetheless, the practice did cross the Atlantic from England.

The earliest report comes from Boston in 1681. A Michael Smith believed that his landlady, a local healer named Mary Hale, had put him under a spell. He went to stay at the house of another cunning woman, Hannah Weacome, seeking a remedy. Weacome placed his urine in a bottle and then locked it in a cabinet. After she did so, Mary Hale showed up at the house and walked about outside it for about an hour, until other women at the house convinced Weacome to unlock the cabinet and to open the bottle. [115]

The Boston minister Increase Mather stated "how persons that shall unbewitch others by putting Urin into a Bottle, or by casting Excrements… can wholly cure themselves from being white Witches, I am not able to understand"[116]. Nine years later, he became more strident in condemning similar practices:

> … there have been ways of trying *Witches* long used in many *Nations*… [but these] were invented by the *Devil*, that so innocent *Persons* might be condemned, and some notorious *Witches* escape: Yea, many Superstitious and Magical experiments have been used to try *Witches* by: Of this sort is

---

115 Godbeer, *The Devil's Dominion*, 45–46; Tannenbaum, *The Healer's Calling*, 126.
116 Mather, *An Essay for the Recording of Illustrious Providences*, 269.

> *that of scratching the Witch, or seething the Urine of the bewitched Person, or making a Witch-cake with that Urine...*[117]

His son Cotton also brought up this remedy for witchcraft, along with some thoughts on the symbolism of the nails:

> *We shall add a Second Instance, wherein I shall Relate something that I do not Approve; and that is, The Urinary Experiment. I suppose the Urine must be bottled with Nails and Pins, and such Instruments in it as carry a shew of Torture with them, if it attain its End. For I have been told, That the bare Bottling of Urine with Filings of Steel in it, which can be better (tho' scarce well) accounted for, has been found insignificant. Now to use a Charm against a Charm... who can with a good Conscience try?*[118]

Mather goes on to describe a man afflicted with witchcraft from Northampton. He had rebuked a servant, who reported the matter to his wife. This woman used her supernatural abilities to cause illness and the appearance of mysterious animals in the master's household. An attempt was made to create a witch bottle for him, but the man's penis had a hole in it that prevented him from filling the bottle, and he died.

Undoubtedly both Mathers, who were intimately involved in the trials at Salem, felt their own brand of witch discovery to be preferable to the bottle charm. Deodat Lawson, a former minister of Salem-Village, agreed. In a sermon said to have been given in the town on March 24, 1692, he warned against such anti-witchcraft measures as "*Burning* the Afflicted Persons hair; parings of Nails, [or] *stopping* up and boyling the Urine."[119]

Witch bottles did come into the proceedings at Salem. One of the accused, Martha Emerson, was cross-examined on July

---

117 Mather, *A Further Account of the Tryals of the New-England Witches*, Part 2, 29.
118 Mather and Baxter, *Late Memorable Providences Relating to Witchcrafts and Possessions*, 59–60.
119 Lawson, *Christ's Fidelity*, 64.

23, 1692, accused of attending the sabbat and afflicting young girls with magical torment. Bizarrely, she was also tried for putting a person's urine in a bottle or glass that was placed in an oven to ward off witchcraft. Her father, who had passed away in prison, had told the judges that she had killed a witch in this manner. Ms. Emerson confessed that she had indeed kept the woman's urine in a glass. (If this was for the purpose of the procedure, this might be our first confirmed glass witch bottle.) In the end, her life was spared.[120]

Six years later, in Great Island, New Hampshire, the family of one George Walton was beset by mysterious falls of stones. Today's readers on the supernatural would attribute this to poltergeists, but witchcraft was suspected at the time. On August 1, the family placed crooked pins and urine in a clay pot over a fire to compel whatever witch was responsible to desist. They performed this operation in a house with stones whizzing through the air, so we can guess the outcome.[121]

LATER EVIDENCE

Given that the geographic expanse of the continent and its relatively rapid settlement, historically speaking, an examination of North American witch bottles is probably best done in terms of space rather than time. Thus, the next part of our exploration will proceed from north to south through the eastern states, after which we will move to points west.

In the fishing villages of Newfoundland, "putting up a bottle" has remained a common remedy for misfortune. Barbara Rieti tells one particularly dramatic story. A local man had two auto tires go flat, and both his wife's wedding ring and his wedding photo split in half, all within a single hour. He placed a

---

120 "Martha Emerson."
121 C[hamberline], *Lithobolia, Or, The Stone-Throwing Devil...*

bottle in the oven to heat; a few hours later, a woman from the other side of the island had to be airlifted to the hospital due to a urinary blockage.[122] Another man held such a bottle over his head as part of a ceremony, thereby killing his sister-in-law.[123] A unique aspect of this tradition is that the witch should be named at the time the bottle is created.[124] Further south, the demolishing of the hobs in a Halifax fireplace turned up a bottle filled with nails, the hair of a cow, parings from a hoof, and Bible passages.[125]

The most northerly tale in the States is set in Warren, New Hampshire, shortly after the American Revolution. A prominent citizen and constable of the town, Simeon Smith, was believed to have magical powers. Smith was feuding with Stevens Merrill, who Smith had compelled to pay taxes to support the American cause. One day Merrill's boy Caleb started to act strangely, sometimes writhing in pain, at other times climbing to the roof of the house or barn. Merrill's neighbours convinced him to place a bottle with Caleb's urine under the hearth. Twice, Smith developed a nosebleed which seemed to last until the cork popped out of the bottle. The third time, Merrill replaced the urine with blood and placed a sword in the cork. This led to the death of Smith, and the alleviation of Caleb's illness.[126]

The staff at the Raitt Homestead Farm Museum in Eliot, Maine reported finding an empty bottle with a pentagram on the cork beneath the house's eaves. The house itself was built in 1896, and the presence of the pentagram suggests this is a more recent production. No further evidence on this item has been forthcoming.[127]

---

122 Rieti, *Making Witches*, 30–1.
123 Ibid., 143.
124 Ibid., 34, 98.
125 Wilkinson, "Local Folk Lore," 6–7.
126 Little, *The History of Warren*, 437–38.
127 Manning, "The Material Culture of Ritual Concealments in the United States," 58.

An early nineteenth-century bottle containing fingernail parings was found near an African-American slave burial ground in Colonie, New York. The Schuyler family, once prominent in New York state politics, once owned this land. Other bottles have been found hidden in Hudson Valley houses, but none have been noted as containing nails or pins, and archaeologists have not analyzed their contents.[128]

Another glass phial, dating to the late eighteenth or early nineteenth centuries, has turned up in an excavation at the Cove Lands near Providence, Rhode Island. Little has been revealed about this bottle, save that it is a clear bottle likely used for medicine, and that six straight pins were inside.[129]

A glass bottle, holding six brass pins and found near a potsherd and a bone (likely that of a bird), was found at Essington, Pennsylvania, at Governor Printz State Park. The bottle dates to approximately 1748, and the Taylors, a Quaker family dwelling near the find's location in the eighteenth century, are believed to have deposited the bottle.[130]

The extent to which the practice had seeped into the country's culture might be demonstrated through its appearance in "powwowing." Despite its name, the practice has little to do with Native American spirituality and medicine, instead being a German-American magical and devotional practice primarily associated with Pennsylvania.

The first powwowing work to discuss witch bottles was *Der Lange Verborgene Freund* (*The Long-Lost Friend*), a book of charms and remedies compiled by John George Hohman, an immigrant from Alsace, in 1820. He provides it as a "remedy to be applied when any one is sick." This might not be a reference to

---

128 Wheeler, "Magical Dwelling," 387.
129 Becker, "An Update on Colonial Witch Bottles," 18.
130 Becker, "An American Witch-bottle"; Becker, "An Eighteenth Century Witch Bottle in Delaware County, Pennsylvania."

mundane maladies, as he often included anti-witchcraft charms in his works under vague labels.

> *Let the sick person, without having conversed with any one, make water in a bottle before sun-rise, close it up tight, and put it immediately in some box or chest, lock it and stop up the key-hole; the key must be carried in one of the pockets for three days, as nobody dare have it except the person who puts the bottle with urine in the chest or box.*[131]

Hohman provides no source for the charm. It might have originated in English sources that became assimilated into the Pennsylvania German community. On the other hand, Hohman's previous homeland was along the Rhine valley, a major site of bellarmine production, so it might be a technique from there that Hohman brought to the States.

Another nineteenth-century Pennsylvania German manual of remedies, *Doctor Helfenstein's Secrets of Sympathy*, provides a variant on Hohman's. This one extends the period of keeping the bottle locked to nine days, and the person is not to lend or to give anything to anyone, and each day, they must say this charm three times a day:

> *Just as Paul was bound, so be thou defeated. In Jesus' name, thou shalt burn, in the name of Peter thou shalt burst. Make good what thou hast harmed, or else the bonds of hell will rest upon thee. Thine heart shall burn in thy body, thy blood shall run away like water. Thou shalt grow lame and crooked, deaf, and dumb. Thy bladder shall burst. In the air thou shalt be scorched, in the name of the Holy Spirit, and the Holy Guardian Angels.*[132]

We see a final printed Pennsylvania variant, also involving a locked container, in *The Guide to Health, or Household Instructor*, published by "Ossman and Steel" in the small town of Wiconisco, Pennsylvania, in 1894. It is a curious hybrid mix of

---

131 Hohman and Harms, *The Long-Lost Friend*, 48.
132 Donmoyer, *Powwowing in Pennsylvania: Braucherei and the Ritual of Everyday Life*, 300.

various procedures used "when one is sick and wasting away in flesh":

> Let the patient without having conversed with anyone, urinate in a new bottle before sunrise in the morning. Then put nine new needles and nine new pins in the bottle, and close as tight as you possibly can and immediately lock the bottle with its contents in a tight box or chest, after which the keyhole must be well closed with bread or putty.
>
> The key, however, must be carried with the person who locked the box or chest shut. Some one will come to loan, but be careful so as not to loan anything from the house, premises, or person within nine days, or this remedy will be in vain. Care must also be taken that nothing is stolen from either of these places.[133]

A charm very similar to this turns last one up over a century later, in the account of Aunt Sophia Bailer, a powwower from Tremont, Pennsylvania. A woman living nearby had the sensation that a figure sat on her chest at night, crushing out her breath. Her husband came to Bailer to ask for a healing. The healer told him to acquire a bottle and fill it with urine before sunrise, followed by nine new needles and nine new pins with their points up. After this, the bottle should be placed in a box, which is then locked, the lock filled with putty, and the key kept on his person. After that, nothing should be loaned to or from the house, and nothing should stand in or out of the house. Not even the laundry should be hanging outside at night. The witch later revealed herself to the couple, asking them to open the box for her. The ending of the story is unclear, but apparently the man later moved to Allentown. The witch seems to have been lucky, as Bailer claimed that, in another case, the use of such a bottle led to the woman's death.[134]

---

133 Ossman and Steel, *The Guide to Health or Household Instructor*, 61; Donmoyer, *Powwowing in Pennsylvania: Braucherei and the Ritual of Everyday Life*, 191.
134 Bailer, "Witches... I Have Known," 8.

On the other end of Pennsylvania, on Market Street in Pittsburgh, a witch bottle was deposited in a garbage pit shortly after 1824. The glass bottle is unusual for including not only a felt heart studded with pins, but also two insoles from a person's shoes. The owners of the property seem to have been English in origin, though some of them had contact with the German Harmonist community. It is also possible that a non-resident left the bottle in the location.[135]

In 1792, Joseph Doddridge became an Episcopal minister, preaching at several congregations around what is today the Northern Panhandle of West Virginia. Taking up medical training as well, he was a keen observer of the medicinal practices of settlers of the region. He mentions in his memoirs that placing a bottle of a child's urine in a chimney was a common anti-witchcraft technique on the frontier at his time.[136]

Another early eighteenth-century bottle excavated at the Dutch fort near Lewes, Delaware, is believed to have contained pins, but its significance was not recognized before it was lost.[137]

Both artefacts and practices involving witch bottles have been found in Maryland. Four seventeenth-century bottles, intact and inverted when placed in the ground near the threshold of a home, were excavated at a site near Solomons, Maryland. In a practice referred to as 'plantin' bottles fur 'em,' a magician would put the hair, fingernail, or clothing of the intended victim in a bottle. The bottle would be left where the person might step over it. If the bottle were uncovered and placed in running water, however, it could be turned back on the caster.[138]

---

135 Alexandrowicz, "The Market Street Witch Bottle"; Becker, "An Update on Colonial Witch Bottles."
136 Doddridge, *Notes on the Settlement*, 180.
137 Becker, "An Update on Colonial Witch Bottles," 17.
138 King, "The Patuxent Point Site," 27–9. Whitney and Bullock, *Folk-Lore from Maryland*, 82–83.

Witch bottles also became part of conjure or hoodoo, a tradition of alternative medicine that was primarily an African-American practice. Although much of its magic came from Africa, some of the charms and magical procedures used within were reinterpreted from European magical traditions.[139] Within this tradition, items like witch bottles seem to have been used to both harm and heal. One possible such item is the neck of a wine bottle, its stopper filled with pins bent and straight, that archaeologists uncovered at a site in Dorchester County, Maryland, that might at one point have served as a slave quarter.[140]

In the nineteenth century, present-day Accomac, Virginia, was once the home of Zippy Tull, a conjure doctor. A young man approached her, believing himself to be cursed. She performed a divination with cards, telling him that a woman was working magic against him and had poisoned his dog. She instructed him to take five or six items, including his "water," new pins and needles, and perhaps some shot, to place them in a bottle, and to hide them in a hole in the fireplace. Within a week, the accused woman showed up at the house, promising to never curse anyone ever again. She died shortly thereafter.[141]

During the Civil War, the Confederacy ordered to be built a set of fortifications, Redoubt 9, between Williamsville and Newport News, Virginia. Later in the conflict, Union troops from Pennsylvania occupied the same structure. Near a hearth in the structure, archaeologists found a blue bottle, from the Charles Grove Company in Columbia, Pennsylvania, filled with nails and with its neck broken. If this is a witch bottle, it could

---

139 Anderson, *Conjure in African American society*. 54-56.
140 Morehouse, "Curator's Choice: Witch Bottle."
141 Hyatt, *Hoodoo--Conjuration--Witchcraft--Rootwork; Beliefs Accepted by Many Negroes and White Persons, These Being Orally Recorded among Blacks and Whites*, vols. 1, 923–5.

be the work of soldiers on either side, or of slaves who built the fortifications.[142]

A volunteer at an archaeological excavation near Virginia Beach turned up a green phial for medicine dating to the first half of the eighteenth century, containing approximately two dozen brass pins and three iron nails. Circumstantial evidence suggests the bottle might be linked to the activities of Grace Sherwood, the eighteenth-century Witch of Pungo, who was imprisoned for witchcraft for nine years.[143]

While in Richmond, Virginia, the teacher and minister David Webster Davis composed a piece on the dangers of alternative medical practitioners working with the African-American community. He presents a hypothetical consultation with a "doctor," who promises to free his client from bewitchment. To do so, the "doctor" must visit their home at midnight, sacrificing a chicken, and then digging up the bewitching bottle, displaying:

> *an ordinary bottle partly covered in the dirt: inside of it is usually found a heterogeneous [sic] mixture of dissimilar articles: - a piece of a knife-blade, pins, curiously bent, broken and rusty needles, pieces of red flannel, red pepper, perhaps a small snake, and whatever the ingenuity of the "doctor" may suggest to mystify and awe the ignorant uninitiated.*[144]

Davis presents this as an object that a charlatan has planted while pretending to dig it up, yet it does possess some of the qualities of an anti-witchcraft item, including the "curiously bent" pins. It is uncertain whether this is a local innovation, or instead represents a misunderstanding on the part of the author.

---

142 Berard, "Civil War-Era Bottle"; Hall, "The Tale of The Civil War Hoodoo Spell Bottle."
143 Painter, "An Early 18th Century Witch Bottle."
144 Davis, "Folk-Lore and Ethnology: Conjuration," 252.

An anonymous individual from Richmond reported another, more traditional use of the witch bottle, to the clergyman Harry Middleton Hyatt. Hyatt travelled through the Southeast from 1936 to 1940, collecting conjure and hoodoo charms, resulting in his massive five-volume compilation *Hoodoo – Conjuration – Witchcraft – Rootwork*. The formula from our Richmond informant required the user to tie together nine pins, four with points up and five down, with a thread. After placing the pin in the bottle with the urine, the creator should go to an abandoned house, hide the bottle behind a brick in the fireplace, speak the phrase, "Bad luck go away, good luck follah," and leave without looking back. The person responsible for the hostile magic will see their designs foiled in nine days.[145]

Another of Hyatt's informants from Wilmington, North Carolina, described how she had corresponded with a man in Washington, DC for several months. He stopped writing after a while, claiming that he was suddenly losing his vision. Upon consulting a conjure doctor, he found that a rival for love was attacking him with magic over jealousy for a previous relationship. The doctor advised him to fill a bottle with his urine just before sunup and place it under the attacker's front step each morning. Having done so for six weeks, he found himself cured, and he eventually married the Wilmington woman.[146]

A woman living near Brushy Fork, North Carolina, circa 1880, was afraid of a potential witch named "Old Henry." Her bed was in the loft of the house, and her parents hung a bottle, stopped tightly, on a string nearby. Keeping the bottle closed was essential to her health. The collector, Dr. Frank C. Brown, did not note what, if anything, the bottle contained.[147]

---

145 Hyatt, *Hoodoo--Conjuration--Witchcraft--Rootwork*, vol. 1, 507-8.
146 Ibid., vol. 1, 508.fff
147 Frank C. Brown Collection of North Carolina Folklore. et al., *The Frank C.*

One nineteenth-century South Carolina client of a conjure doctor became convinced that witches were leaving dangerous material on his property to injure him. Digging up some knotted horsehair and a coffin-shaped piece of wood, he placed these in a bottle to capture the witch. The authorities were called in when he called upon his followers to patrol his property with guns as another anti-witchcraft measure. Although the man was clearly unstable, his practice echoes those from centuries before.[148]

In 1877, a folklore collector visited the Proctor family, living near Savannah, Georgia. The family had buried iron nails in a black bottle under their doorstep, to ward off witches.[149]

Ray Browne collected witch bottle traditions during his work in Alabama. If a person knew who was casting evil magic at them, they might put urine and pins in a bottle, which was then put into a chimney to reverse it. Another charm involved the person reciting the names of potential witches while dismantling the bricks in a fireplace. A bottle of water would be buried in ashes, and the first person who visited was the witch.[150]

Archaeologists working at the Armstrong Farmstead in Fayette County, Kentucky, uncovered a corked glass bottle with four pins within, near an early nineteenth-century structure. It might be another example of a witch bottle, but it is difficult to be certain.[151]

Early settlers in Union County, Illinois, brought their beliefs in witches with them to their new homes. Those who suspected witchcraft was afflicting someone could reverse the spell by bottling the person's urine and hanging it in the chimney. The witch became afflicted with strangury, alleviated only if the

---

Brown Collection of North Carolina Folklore, 646.
148 Babcock, "Communicated Insanity," 519–520.
149 Ruby Andrews Moore, "Superstitions in Georgia."
150 Browne, *Popular Beliefs and Practices from Alabama.*, 195, 198.
151 Manning, "Homemade Magic," 114–15.

witch could borrow something from the household, or if someone removed the bottle.[152]

Hyatt began his folklore collection work in Adams County, Illinois – although the following story he was told took place in Iowa. Mr. W., a conjure doctor, called upon a woman because she was so ill she couldn't walk. Mr. W. located a ball of rags and a small bottle of liquid under the woman's porch. When he poured liquid from his own magic bottle into the other, it exploded, revealing a small number of needles. Fortunately, he still had the ball of rags, which he filled with the needles and tossed in the fire. Shortly thereafter, the sick woman walked out to ask him what he wanted.[153]

Witch bottles even made it to the west coast. During a recent archaeological excavation to rebuild the Cypress Expressway in West Oakland after the earthquake of 2005, a bottle with a needle-studded cork and yet-to-be-determined contents turned up at the home of a German family.[154]

We have a few examples from the Caribbean as well. This item, collected in the Bahamas in the early years of the twentieth century, is worth quoting at length:

> *If you think you are hagged*[155]*, get quickly some of your water into a bottle (there are differences as to the proper size, form, and color; the majority advocate a wide-mouthed black bottle); don't spill one drop; put in also some guinea pepper, several new needles and pins - not more than six of each - and cork it tight; this will give you power over the hag, and keep her from making water. The first person you will see in the morning will be your hag, who will beg of you bread, or something else, just to make you talk; if you do talk, you will loosen her, and she will be free; otherwise, if you keep your mouth shut, and wish to make her suffer, she will be obliged*

---

152 Perrin, *History of Alexander, Union and Pulaski Counties, Illinois*, 281.
153 Hyatt, *Folk-Lore from Adams County, Illinois*, 798.
154 Gibson, "Crosses and Witch Bottles."
155 Bewitched.

> *to come to you, until you speak to her and free her from the spell. If you mean to kill her, never speak a word to her, and after a while her bladder will burst, and she will die. If you prefer to kill her in another way, throw the corked bottle into the sea, and she will go and drown herself.*[156]

This was inverted in other cases, when a magician seeking to harm a person buried a bottle with urine, unspecified herbs, and needles near their dwelling.[157]

Sir Henry Hesketh Joudou Bell, who would later become the first governor of Uganda, spent his early administrative career in the West Indies. He describes the following example from his time there, most likely taken from Grenada. To prevent the theft of plantains from a field, a local practitioner placed bottles hanging in trees nearby.

> *Going to one of the trees, he untied one of the mysterious bottles and opened it. 'Just look! this vial contains nothing but sea-water, with a little laundry blue in it, and, as you can see, a dead cockroach floating on the top. They nearly all contain almost the same things, some may have besides the cockroach, a few rusty nails and a bit of red flannel or suchlike rubbish. …the unfortunate thief would inevitably come to a bad end, very shortly; in fact, 'swell up and bust'…*[158]

During excavations at the Juan de Bolas plantation on Jamaica in 2002-4, archaeologist Matthew Reeves and his chief assistant Linton Rhule found two upright wine bottles in the yard. Rhule commented that similarly-placed bottles served as "duppy bottles" buried as part of Obeah practice. Such a bottle could include nail parings for binding that person's soul to a nearby cotton tree, or their hair to ensure destruction, although other combinations could have beneficial effects. Such items

---

156 Clavel, "Items of Folk-Lore from Bahama Negroes," 36–37.
157 Wilkie, "Secret and Sacred: Contextualizing the Artifacts of African-American Magic and Religion," 88.
158 Bell, *Obeah*, 4–5.

could be buried in the yard, near a corner, or in proximity to a gate.[159]

The clergyman Charles Kingsley spent the winter of 1869-70 in the West Indies. During his trip, he attended the trial of a local Obeah practitioner. The man had offered a servant to bury "a bottle containing toad, spider, rusty nails, dirty water, and other terrible jumbiferous articles" near the house of the warden in order to afflict him, only to have the servant turn him in.[160]

---

[159] Reeves, "Mundane or Spiritual?," 185–86.
[160] Kingsley, At Last, 236.

Today's Witch Bottles

Those peering into the cases at the Pitt Rivers Museum at Oxford might see a small bottle of silvered glass, stoppered with cork and wax. It was first seen in possession of an old woman in Hove, Sussex, in 1915, who is quoted as saying, 'They do say there be a witch in it, and if you let him out there'll be a peck o' trouble.' This could be a witch bottle, or an item intended to catch a spirit – frankly, no one seems to be willing to flout the woman's prohibition. In either case, the bottle was donated to the museum in 1926 by Margaret Murray, whose works, *The Witch-Cult in Western Europe* and *The God of the Witches* did much to inspire Gerald Gardner's creation of Wicca and, from there, the rise of modern Paganism.[161]

Bottle in the Pitt Rivers Collection

If the Pitt Rivers object is a witch bottle, it would certainly represent the next stage of the bottle tradition: its transmission from primarily lower-class and artisan Christian village practitioners serving their communities, to a more middle-class group seeking magical techniques they could practice in private as part of the reconstruction of a Pagan faith. The first group was more likely to learn their craft from the transmission of

---

161 MJD and Pitt Rivers Museum, "1926.6.1: Glass Flask Reputed to Contain a Witch."

books and oral teachings, while the second are active participants in a market for both knowledge and spiritual goods. I acknowledge that some individuals or groups might not adhere strictly to either of these two categories, but I think these rough categories convey a fundamental change in how witch bottles were perceived and utilized.

It is not clear how knowledge of witch bottles was transferred. Given the overlap between their devotees and those interested in folklore, it is likely that the practice could easily have been gleaned from the journals of the time. This should not rule out the possibility that the techniques were passed on orally in some instances. No matter the exact line of transmission, witch bottles have been revived and become part of the conjuring toolkit of today's witches, pagans, and others interested in the magical arts.

It might be appropriate here to comment on the witch bottle collection collected by Cecil Williamson (1909-1999), which became part of the Museum of Witchcraft and Magic, now in Boscastle, Cornwall. The museum has an array of such items, ranging from the era of bellarmine use to creations of modern witches, and some that include unusual elements such as chicken wing feathers and coloured threads. The latter suggests what Nigel Pennick has referred to as the "Cambridgeshire witch bottle," green or bluish-green bottles filled with threads, often red, and placed over a house's door. None of the museum's bottles are precisely dated, so it is hoped that archaeologists will examine them soon.[162]

Williamson also was a keen collector of local folkloric practice, and Gemma Gary relays a rite he witnessed that was

---

162 Museum of Witchcraft and Magic, "14 - Witch Bottle: Bellarmine Jar"; Museum of Witchcraft and Magic, "221 - Witch Bottle: Bellarmine Jar"; Museum of Witchcraft and Magic, "1438 - Witch Bottle"; Museum of Witchcraft and Magic, "1830 - Spirit Bottle: Witch Bottle"; Pennick, *Skulls, Cats, and Witch Bottles*, 18.

intended to change an individual's behaviour. After the entrances and windows are taped shut, a pot of water and a variety of plants (in one case, including cabbage, dandelion, groundsel, and verbena) is boiled. Next, a bottle of urine is cast into the pot, boiling until it explodes. This causes stomach pains in the person, who calls upon a local "white witch" who explains that the situation might be a result of the person's behaviour.[163]

Many different varieties of charms are found in contemporary hoodoo, with nine pins, nine needles, and nine coffin nails becoming the key ingredients instead of urine, along with graveyard dirt, faeces, menstrual blood, "hot foot powder," semen, or various minerals and plants associated with evil power. The bottle charm has lost most of its protective and countermagical significance, now being used to inflict injury and weakness upon a victim.[164]

Witch bottles have also become part of the traditions of Wicca in America, through the works of Scott Cunningham and David Harrington. The two authors ask their readers to fill a bottle with rosemary and red wine in addition to sharp objects, while reciting:

> *Pins, needles, rosemary and wine.*
> *In this Witch's Bottle of mine;*
> *Guard against harm and enmity;*
> *This is my will, so mote it be!*[165]

Charms with these ingredients have seen a wide dissemination through Pagan sites on the internet and contemporary books on the topic, even though the inclusion of rosemary and wine has not been noted in any sources before

---

163 Gary, *Wisht Waters*, 101–2.
164 Puckett, "Folk Beliefs of the Southern Negro," 299; Yronwode, "Witch's Bottle (Malevolent, Not Protective)"; Yronwode, "Witch Bottles: Hoodoo and British."
165 Cunningham and Harrington, *The Magical Household*, 107.

this time.[166] Other recent charms, bringing together such ingredients with other herbs, coins, and shiny objects, are used to provide protection and prosperity to a household, or to stop bullying.[167] Many of these are quite different from the bottles we have seen previously. The most faithful to the original, including a dark-coloured bottle, sharp objects, and urine, appears in an anti-hexing work, but even this is buried at the edge of the property and not a more traditional location.[168]

On a trip years ago to Salem, I purchased a witch bottle from a local shop. The creators had discarded most of the traditional aspects of the practice. The small bottle does contain one nail and salt, but it also incorporates Salem dirt, clove, and – of course – rosemary, along with a "Domus Defendio" charm. Those with this bottle may be able to keep "Hearth & Home safe from the Destructive Forces of Evil & Malicious Spirits," although the label also warns that it "makes no claims of preventing Sickness or Misfortune." I purchased mine for $8.95.

We have at least one case of a witch bottle of more questionable origins. In June of 2009, an inspector and two constables of the Ontario Provincial Police were evicting a young man from a campsite. Among his effects was a plastic bottle, with sharp screws protruding from the cap, which he said was filled with razor blades and urine to protect him from "bad people."[169]

---

166 e.g. Canard, *Defences Against the Witches' Craft*, 65–66; TipToeChick, "How to Make a Witch Bottle."; Furie, *Supermarket Sabbats*, 55–56, 77–78, 116–18, 135–36, 221–22, 262.
167 Weinstein, *Earth Magic*, 131-3; TipToeChick, "How to Make a Witch Bottle."
168 Chauran, *Have You Been Hexed?*, 152–3.
169 Andrews, "Bottles and Blades."

Witch Bottles in the Media

As witch bottles grow in popularity, they have also seeped into popular media. I have done little examination of their roles in literary fiction, so I will leave this to others.

The first appearance of a witch bottle in visual media might have been September 17, 1975, in "The Witch's Bottle," the third episode of the Thames Television series *Shadows*. The episode, written by the Wiccan high priest and author Stewart Farrar, does include a bottle, but as a container for the energy of a witch, similar to the Pitt Rivers Museum bottle.[170]

The first movie, to my knowledge, to feature a witch bottle was *The Love Witch* (2016). In one scene, the witch Elaine (Samantha Robinson) creates a witch bottle. She puts in the traditional ingredients of nails and urine, as well as the rosemary typical of modern witch bottles and a used tampon. She then leaves this on top of the grave of her murdered lover for reasons that remain unclear.[171]

A short film, entitled *Tales of Churel: Dead Water*, appeared in 2017 with the alternate title "Witch Bottle." It follows a girl working on a farm, played by Rinya Cyrus, who finds a mysterious sealed bottle next to her house. She accidentally breaks it, thereafter seeing visions of a mysterious figure. She researches witch bottle folklore to reveal the source of the shocking visions appearing around her:

> *Witch bottle: Protection against a witch's curse. They were used to trap spells cast by witches. They were over pieced together in glass bottles or vials containing charms. Other*

---

170 Hughes, "Shadows."
171 Biller, *The Love Witch*.

> *elements in the bottle consisted of rusty nails, glass or mirror fragments, and even the urine or menstrual blood of the victim. Witch bottles were often placed in the structure of the building or buried beneath the house. It was believed that the bottle would capture and impale evil on the sharp objects found inside. Witch bottles were supposedly active until the bottle was broken.*[172]

This is surprisingly accurate – the only element that does not seem to be present in other sources is the mirror, and the use of the sharp objects to "capture and impale evil" is plausible.

---

172 Golding, *Witch Bottle*.

Discussion

The witch bottle is one of a wide range of traditional anti-witchcraft charms, including the heating of milk to overcome witchcraft against cattle, the baking of cakes involving the person's urine, or the insertion of pins into a heart which is then injured or placed in the chimney. Witch bottles were quite popular; the ingredients were cheap and readily available, it was said to provide immediate relief from whatever condition was necessary, and, unlike other anti-witchcraft charms such as bleeding, it usually did not require the user to know the name of the suspected witch or to contact the person.

GEOGRAPHY

New documentation or discoveries might extend our knowledge of the range of witch bottles. From the earliest period, witch bottles seem to have been a phenomenon of eastern England, with bellarmines being the most common receptacles used. The largest number of these come from Norfolk, though whether this reflects the prevalence of the custom or issues relating to discovery or reporting is unknown[173]. Many bottles are found in Sussex, London, and Essex. Oddly enough, few examples of bottles from later periods are found in London proper.

Over time, the use of witch bottles slowly spread outward. By the nineteenth century, the practice had travelled north to Yorkshire. We have few reports from the western counties of England, suggesting that the practice never became widespread there. The exception is Cornwall, in which we see a spate of discoveries of bottles from the nineteenth century, with usage

---

[173] Hoggard, "The Archaeology of Folk Magic."

dropping off by the twentieth. More distant areas seem to have seen little use of the practice. We have reports from Wales, Ireland, and Scotland, though these are hardly enough to establish a pattern.

We cannot know all the factors that led to the dissemination of the practice. Cunning folk, the practitioners of magic often consulted for cases of illness, theft, or love, seem to be crucial individuals in passing on such information.[174] Although other medical and magical practitioners of various social groups did disseminate the technique, cunning folk are referred to repeatedly in the witch trial accounts and the folklore as the purveyors of the rite to those in need. We might also consider popular literature as another factor. Blagrave's recipe seems to be the only explicit set of instructions published, but many people could have become aware of the basics of the technique through the printed narratives of witchcraft prosecutions. Nonetheless, there is much we do not know about the transmission of this knowledge, especially when it comes to the bottles buried beneath houses.

COMPONENTS

The first item of significance for a bottle is the container itself. In the earliest reports, this might have simply been a pot or pan in which the other substances could be placed to be boiled. By the seventeenth century, bellarmines became more common, whether due to their ubiquity or the striking face rendered on their necks. Within our surviving corpus, as examined by Brian Hoggard, over half of the bottles found and identified have been bellarmines. They appear almost entirely or near ports on the river or sea, areas that would have seen such bottles imported in high numbers. In the eighteenth century,

---

174 Davies, *Cunning-folk*.

bellarmines were less used in general, and various glass phials and bottles came into use, with the type chosen usually being one of the cheaper vessels available. Still, Bellhouse's work shows that, even in the nineteenth century, a pan could still be used for this purpose. Such rites, or those similar, continued to be practiced into the twentieth century.[175]

The next key ingredient is often urine, though we have some uncertainty as to how often it appears. First, many of the folklore collectors of the nineteenth century do not mention it explicitly, possibly due to inhibitions about reporting elements seen as vulgar. Second, urine has proved to be a difficult compound to test for, in the rare cases in which the liquid from the discovered bottles survived and was kept preserved for testing. As such, archaeologists have been cautious about pronouncing the liquid in these bottles to be urine. A 2009 laboratory analysis confirmed its presence in a seventeenth-century bottle, laying the ground for more examinations.[176] Lest it appear that archaeologists have been overcautious on declaring the contents to be urine, the example from William Drage indicates that a similar procedure might have been used against bewitchment of other liquids.

Along the same principles of contagious magic, other portions of the body of the bewitched might also be added. Among these might be hair (often from the nape of the neck), blood, and nail parings, or possibly hair and hoof parings if livestock were concerned.

The third major ingredients were sharp metal objects – pins, needles, or nails, with thorns being substituted at times. These could be placed free in the bottle, stuck through another object, or inserted into the cork or stopper itself. These serve as a key

---

175 Hoggard, "Witch Bottles: Their Contents, Contexts and Uses," 98–99; Thwaite, "Magic and the Material Culture of Healing," 228; "Fulbourn Man's Superstition.'"
176 Pitts, "Urine to Navel Fluff."

indicator of discovered witch bottles, as these are usually one of the few ingredients to survive or leave traces. Whereas liquid is rarely found in a bottle, as of 2004 iron had been found in 90% of the reported bottles, and in almost every bottle with contents noted.[177]

The number of pins in a bottle often varies considerably, and many of them seem to be bent or curved deliberately before placement within. Hoggard notes that, despite the lack of any instructions to bend the pins, such items are found in almost all archaeological examples. He suggests that the pins are present because the witch is fooled into believing the person's heart is inside, injuring themselves on the pins in the process[178]. This does not explain those examples in which the bottle is heated, or other sources drawing analogies with the bladder. It might also be due to the power over the supernatural traditionally ascribed to iron. Pins have several links to witches, whether as a means for them to do harm, or to uncover or cease their magical activities.[179] We can assume that the pins being bent is a ritual element, as bending them would make their placement within the bottle more difficult. In the nineteenth century, bent pins were often associated with magic; we have one charm in which a bent pin was cast into a fire, as well as multiple holy wells into which crooked pins were cast.[180] Thwaite suggests that crooked pins were generally viewed as negative, but gained a positive association when symbolically removed from the body – whether into a well or a bottle.[181]

---

177 Hoggard, "Witch Bottles: Their Contents, Contexts and Uses," 100; Hoggard, "The Archaeology of Counter-Witchcraft and Popular Magic," 172.
178 Hoggard, 100; Hoggard, "The Archaeology of Folk Magic." He also suggests that these bent items may be "killed" to become "ghost pins," a possibility not documented in the accounts above.
179 Longman and Loch, *Pins and Pincushions*. 30-39.
180 Cuming, "Pin-Lore and the Waxen Image." 163-64; Hope, *Holy Wells of England*, 22, 72, 103, 109, 199.
181 Thwaite, "Magic and the Material Culture of Healing," 139, 154.

Less common, but still notable, are hearts, whether taken from an animal or made of cloth. One-tenth of the bottles reported by 2004 included a cloth heart, with no indication of how many others might have had either sort of heart before it decayed.[182] If the sixteenth-century examples are any indication, animal hearts were the original ingredients, with the cloth hearts being substituted later, possibly due to ease of insertion. In either case, these substances are unlikely to survive for centuries in these bottles, so finding evidence of them in the discovered witch bottles has been difficult.

Other less-common ingredients include salt, plant matter, linen cloth, bird bones, animal bones, pottery, forks, glass, wooden spills or carved objects, brass studs, lint, gunpowder, shoe soles, effigies, and the curious concoction of acids and herbs mentioned in Bellhouse's notebook.

In addition to the type of items, the number added might have special significance. Auge notes that, when multiple discrete items are included in a recipe, they often appear in groups of three or multiples thereof.[183] As we have seen above, odd numbers, especially nine, often turn up in the instructions.

Dr. Manning recently developed an overall typology for American witch bottles based on their contents. Some of the bottles described herein might not fit perfectly into each category, but it provides a convenient summary of much of the data.[184]

---

182 Hoggard, "The Archaeology of Counter-Witchcraft and Popular Magic," 172.
183 Auge, "Silent Sentinels," 115–16.
184 Manning, "Homemade Magic: Concealed Deposits in Architectural Contexts in the Eastern United States," 123. Thanks to Dr. Manning for allowing this to be republished.

Type	Container	Contents	Special Treatment
A-1	Ceramic jug	Urine	
A-2	Glass wine / case bottle		
A-3	Glass vial / steeple bottle		
B-1	Ceramic jug	Pins, needles, nails (usually with urine)	
B-2	Glass wine/case bottle		
B-3	Glass vial		
B-4	Pot, pan, or other open vessel	Pins, needles, nails (usually with urine)	Boiled over fire
C	Ceramic or glass jug, bottle, or vial	Cloth or leather heart pierced with pins/nails	
D	Ceramic or glass jug, bottle, or vial	Any combination of urine, pins, needles, and nails	Pins and needles stuck into the cork
E	Ceramic or glass jug, bottle, or vial	Contents other than urine, pins, needles, and nails	
F	Ceramic or glass jug, bottle, or vial	Empty or containing only water	Concealed in a structure

Manning's Typology of American Witch Bottles

RITUAL

Several accounts portray the rituals that surrounded the creation of the witch bottle. Some of these relate to bottles to be placed in the fire, and they often include lengthy verbal charms not given in the other material. The versions in Blagrave's account and Sloane 3846 are particularly noteworthy, as they suggest an astrological timing to the ritual that does not appear elsewhere.

One element turning up in several accounts is the use of silence as part of the ritual. The practitioner must place the bottle in the fire in silence and resist the witch's distractions, lest the charm be lost. This reflects the severing of the connections of language and physical proximity that bring us together in society, symbolically casting the suspected person out of social networks and their power.

Still, it bears noting that most accounts include no mention of any incantation, and certainly no trace could be found with any archaeological finds. Does this mean that some commentators omitted these, either because they knew none, or because they thought it inappropriate? Were the words not passed on because they were said too quietly to be heard? Or were the ritual components and actions considered sufficient? It is likely that all these possibilities have some degree of truth, although we might never know the exact proportions of each.

USAGE

In most cases, witch bottles are used in two ways: placed in a fire to cause pain to the witch, or buried beneath the ground. The two usages, Glanvil's case aside, seem to be mutually exclusive, as few signs of heat have been noticed on the buried bottles.

One question that remains unresolved is whether the buried bottles might have had a different purpose than fighting witches. Much of the literature has suggested they were used for a more general protective purpose, but Thwaite observes that little contemporary literature connects these items with such purposes.[185] Still, other apotropaic processes, such as the deposition of cats and shoes in walls, have little literature surrounding them. Further, the deposition of the bottles from

---

185 Thwaite, "What Is a 'Witch Bottle'?," 232.

East Anglia beneath the house before it was constructed, or when substantial alterations would need to be made, indicates they were unlikely to be intended for a specific case of witchcraft.[186] Then again, the examples from conjure practice might make us wonder if the owner of the house was always the one who made the deposit. We can hope that further study will help to illuminate this feature.

Hoggard provides two possible explanations for the symbolism of the bottles. First, the bottle could be seen a symbolic bladder, with the contents depicting the injuries desired to be inflicted on the witch. (On the other hand, Davies and Easton find that nineteenth-century sources often give the heart of the witch as the target.) Second, the bottles might have been used as spirit traps in some examples, capturing the spiritual force of the hostile magician and subjecting it to torture.[187]

Some individual accounts also include other details in the practice not seen above. Out of the examples above, we might add observing the movement of the pins in hope of viewing the identity of the witch, or establishing its efficacy by a certain number of needles moving or the appearance of a rainbow of colours. All of these may be later innovations, after the opaque bellarmine bottles had been replaced with clear glass. If the burial of a bottle with the livestock in Yaddlethorpe is no coincidence, the internment might be a means of revenge instead of reflecting a charm.

Some of the evidence from later times indicates that bottles might also be used to place a curse, as the examples above from Dorset, Maryland, and Iowa indicate. These are less common, likely due to the conception behind the magic. The traditional

---

186 Merrifield, *The Archaeology of Ritual and Magic*, 182.
187 Davies and Easton, "Cunning-Folk and the Production of Magical Artefacts," 211; Hoggard, "Witch Bottles: Their Contents, Contexts and Uses," 103–4.

witch bottle assumes that the magic it fights against has already established a connection between the magician and the victim, a connection that the witch bottle can follow back to the point of origination. Thus, a similar spell used as a means of magical attack must have an additional component linking it to the victim, such as being hidden on the victim's property or path.

Finally, we might briefly note the Cornish examples of witch bottles being used as anti-wart charms. As the bottles were not elsewhere associated with warts, it raises the question as to whether this arose from the belief that the warts were caused by hostile magic.

LOCATION

For those bottles not placed in a fire, the creators often deposited them in various areas. The vast majority have been located within the home. Half the discovered witch bottles have been discovered under hearths, and that number rises to four-fifths when we include those found under walls, doorways, or floors.[188] Others, especially the seventeenth-century examples from London, were placed in marginal areas, such as ditches, rivers, and parish boundaries. We have a few other anomalies, such as the two finds in graves mentioned above, and the Pennsylvania German recipes in which the bottle is locked in a chest.

The hearth is an interesting area for the deposit of an item. As the source of heating for cooking and warmth, it served as the centre of the household. Yet the fire that occupied it was also a source of danger, as an unwatched pot or stray spark could destroy a family's home and possessions. Further, the chimney could not be closed, leaving it as a possible point of

---

188 Hoggard, "The Archaeology of Counter-Witchcraft and Popular Magic," 173.

ingress for intruders – including witches and their servants.[189] If we emphasize this final aspect, then it seems witch bottles were deposited in liminal areas of the household that the inhabitants considered boundaries with the less predictable world outside.

A frequent assumption in archaeological literature is that the owners of the property placed the buried witch bottles. Although we should be cautious about connecting data centuries and oceans apart, the accounts collected by Hyatt have similar objects being placed at the home of one's enemy, or in a deserted house.

One common element that appears in most accounts is the burying of the bottle bottom up. This is common enough that finding an intact bottle buried in this position is seen as a prime indication that it might have been a witch bottle. Inversion of conventional orientations and procedures is a common element of many magical procedures, signifying that the actions stand outside of everyday life.

---

189 Easton, "Four Spiritual Middens in Mid Suffolk, England," 10–11.

Conclusion

With the growing interest in, awareness of, and desire to create witch bottles, it is inevitable that this book will be out of date even before it is published. Even in the brief time between these two editions, more bottles have been found and scholars have done much important scholarly work, a trend likely to continue.

One encouraging development has been "Witch Bottles Concealed and Revealed," a collaboration among the Museum of London Archaeology, the University of Hertfordshire, and the Arts and Humanities Research Council, that will extend into 2022. The project is dedicated to collecting, analyzing, and publishing evidence regarding seventeenth-century witch bottles. The project suggests that any witch bottles discovered be reported to the local county museum. Ideally any such item should also be left where it is found, without touching or opening it – although data on moved or opened items is still of interest.[190]

Even for those not in the United Kingdom, I think these are excellent suggestions. Witch bottles are rapidly becoming part of the heritage, not just of one person, but of the world, and granting them to our public institutions and museums will do much to help us to unlock their meaning, to the people of both the past and present.

---

190 Jeffries, "What Should You Do If You Find a 17th-Century 'Witch Bottle'?"

Works Consulted

An Abridged Catalogue of the Saffron Walden Museum. n.p.: Saffron Walden, 1845.
Adshead, Harold. "Canewdon and Its Witches." *Essex Countryside* (1953-54).
Alexandrowicz, J. Stephen. "The Market Street Witch Bottle, Pittsburgh, Pennsylvania." *Proceedings of the Symposium on Ohio Valley Urban and Historic Archaeology* 4 (1986): 117–132.
Amery, P. F. S. "A Witch's Bottle." *Report and Transactions of the Devonshire Association for the Advancement of Science, Literature and Art* 32 (1900): 89–90.
Anderson, Jeffrey E. *Conjure in African American Society*. Baton Rouge: Louisiana State University Press, 2007.
Andrews, Mark. "Bottles and Blades." *British Archaeology* 108 (2009).
Anonymous. *An Account of the Tryal and Examination of Joan Buts, for Being a Common Witch and Inchantress, before the Right Honourable Sir Francis Pemberton, Lord Chief Justice, at the Assizes Holden for the Burrough of Southwark and County of Surrey, on Monday, March 27. 1682*. London: printed for S. Gardener, 1682.
———. *A Miraculous Cure for Witchcraft, or, Strange News from the Blew-Boar in Holburn to the Tune of, Aim Not Too High*. s.l.: s.n., 1670.
———. *Strange and Wonderful News from Goswell-Street: Or, a Victory over the Devil, Being a True Relation How a Person, Living at the House of Francis Jordan at the Sign of the Hunsman and Hounds, near Mount-Mill in Goswell-Street, Having for Three Years Last Past Lain under an Evil-Tongue and Lamentable Fits, Generally Judged to Proceed from Witchcraft, and Was in a Lamentable Condition, and Her Flesh Was as If It Were Tore off Her Bones. With the Strange Noises Heard at That Time, and How the Spirit Struck the Man of the House a Grievous Blow on the Head, Which for Some Hours Occasion'd Great Pain to Him, but Now He Is Recovered. The Truth of This Relation Is and Will Be Attested by Francis Jordan at the Sign of the Hunsman and Hounds, near Mount Mill Aforesaid. Susan Shawe. Margaret Flamstead. Rachel Hopkins. Ralph Jordan. And Several Other Persons. With Allowance*. London: Printed for D.M., 1678.
———. *The True Narrative of the Proceedings at the Session-House in the Old-Bayly, Which Began on Thursday the 1st of This Instant June and Ended on Fryday the 2d. Following Giving an Account of Most of the Remarkable Trials There, Viz. for Murder, Fellonies, and Burglaries, &c. with a Particular Relation of Their Names, and the Places of Their Committing Their Facts, with the Number of Those Condemned to Die, Burned in the Hand, Transported, and to Be Whipt*. London: Printed for L.C., 1682.
———. "Witchcraft in Sussex." *Sussex Archaeological Collections, Relating to the History and Antiquities of the Country* 60 (1919): 147.
Aubrey, John. *Miscellanies* ... London: Printed for Edward Castle, 1696.
Auge, C. Riley. "Silent Sentinels: Archaeology, Magic, and the Gendered Control of Domestic Boundaries in New England, 1620-1725." University of Montana Missoula, 2013. http://scholarworks.umt.edu/etd/884.
Babcock, J. W. "Communicated Insanity and Negro Witchcraft." *The American Journal of Insanity* 51 (May 1894): 518–523.
Bailer, Sophia. "Witches... I Have Known." *The Pennsylvania Dutchman* 4, no. 1 (1952): 8–9.

Bang, Anton Christian. *Norske Hexeformularer og magiske Opskrifter* ... Kristiania: J. Dybwad, 1901.

Becker, M. J. "An Eighteenth Century Witch Bottle in Delaware County, Pennsylvania." *Pennsylvania Archaeologist* 48, no. 1/2 (1978): 1–11.

Becker, Marshall. "An American Witch-bottle." *Archaeology* 33, no. 2 (1980): 18–23.

Becker, Marshall Joseph. "An Update on Colonial Witch Bottles." *Pennsylvania Archaeologist* 75, no. 2 (2005): 12–23.

Bell, Hesketh. *Obeah: Witchcraft in the West Indies*. London: S. Low, Marston & Co., 1893.

Bellhouse, William Dawson. "A Complete System of Magic." New York, 1852.

Berard, Adrienne. "Civil War-Era Bottle Found on Highway Median Maybe Rare 'Witch Bottle.'" William and Mary, January 22, 2020. www.wm.edu/news/stories/2020/civil-war-era-jug-found-on-highway-median-may-be-rare-witch-bottle.php.

Beresford, W. "Notes on a Portion of the Northern Borders of Staffordshire." *The Reliquary* 7 (July 1866): 100–103.

"'Bewitching' a Young Man: Remarkable Case at Brierley Hill." *Birmingham Daily Post*, March 20, 1894.

Biller, Anna. *The Love Witch*. Oscilloscope, 2016.

Blagrave, Joseph. *Blagraves Astrological Practice of Physick Discovering the True Way to Cure All Kinds of Diseases and Infirmities... Being Performed by Such Herbs and Plants Which Grow within Our Own Nation...: Also a Discovery of Some Notable Phylosophical Secrets Worthy Our Knowledge, Relating to a Discovery of All Kinds of Evils, Whether Natural or ... from Sorcery or Witchcraft, or by Being Possessed of an Evil Spirit, Directing How to Cast Forth the Said Evil Spirit Out of Any One Which Is Possessed, with Sundry Examples Thereof*. London: Printed by S.G. and B.G. for Obad. Blagrave ..., 1671.

Boberg, Inger M., ed. *Danske Folketro Samlet Af Jens Kamp*. Danmarks Folkeminder 51. Copenhagen: Foreningen Danmarks Folkeminder, 1943.

Bogg, Edmund. *Lower Wharfeland: The Old City of York and the Ainsty, the Region of Historic Memories: Being a Description of Its Picturesque Features, History, Antiquities, Rare Architecture, Legendary Lore, and Its Flora: Two Hundred Illustrations Prepared Expressly for This Work*. York: J. Sampson, 1904.

Bohak, Gideon. *Ancient Jewish Magic: A History*. Cambridge, UK; New York: Cambridge University Press, 2008.

Bottrell, William. *Traditions and Hearthside Stories of West Cornwall*. Penzance, 1870.

Braekman, Willy Louis. *Magische Experimenten en Toverpraktijken üt een Middelnederlands Handschrift: with an English Summary*. Gent (Belgie): Seminarie voor Volkskunde, 1966.

Bragge, F. *A Full and Impartial Account of the Discovery of Sorcery and Witchcraft Practis'd by Jane Wenham of Walkerne in Hertfordshire...: Also Her Tryal at the Assizes at Hertford ... the Fifth Edition [Witchcraft Farther Display'd...: The Case of the Hertfordshire Witchcraft Consider'd: Being an Examination of a Book Entitl'd A Full and Impartial Account of the Discovery of Sorcery & Witchcraft Practis'd by Jane Wenham of Walkern ...]*. London: Printed for E. Curll: Printed for John Pemberton, 1712.

Brindle, Tom. "Record ID: NARC-0ACAB1 - POST MEDIEVAL Witch Bottle." *Portable Antiquities Scheme*, March 1, 2005. http://finds.org.uk/database/artefacts/record/id/121047.

British Broadcasting Corporation. "Ancient Anti-Witchcraft Potion Found at Old Northamptonshire Pub." *British Broadcasting Company*, October 31, 2019. www.bbc.com/news/uk-england-northamptonshire-50186758.

Browne, Ray B. *Popular Beliefs and Practices from Alabama*. Berkeley: University of California Press, 1958.

Buckinghamshire County Museum Archaeological Service. *Archaeological Investigations at All Saints Church, Loughton, Milton Keynes*. Halton: County Museum Technical Centre, 1994.

Campbell, John Gregorson. *Witchcraft & Second Sight in the Highlands & Islands of Scotland: Tales and Traditions Collected Entirely from Oral Sources*. J. MacLehose & Sons: Glasgow, 1902.

Canard, John. *Defences Against the Witches' Craft*. London: Avalonia, 2008.

C[hamberline], R[ichard]. *Lithobolia, Or, The Stone-Throwing Devil Being an Exact and True Account (by Way of Journal) of the Various Actions of Infernal Spirits, or (devils Incarnate) Witches, or Both, and the Great Disturbance and Amazement They Gave to George Waltons Family, at a Place Call'd Great Island in the Province of New-Hantshire in New-England* ... London: Printed, and are to be sold by E. Whitlook ..., 1698.

Chauran, Alexandra. *Have You Been Hexed?: Recognizing and Breaking Curses*, 2013.

Clavel, M. "Items of Folk-Lore from Bahama Negroes." *The Journal of American Folklore* 17, no. 64 (January 1, 1904): 36–38.

Copson, Chris. "A Witch Bottle from 1 Grove Lane, Stalbridge." *Proceedings of the Dorset Natural History and Archaeological Society* 117 (1995): 142.

Cuming, H. Syer. "Pin-Lore and the Waxen Image." *Journal of the British Archaeological Association* 5. New Series (1899): 161–170.

Cunningham, Scott, and David Harrington. *The Magical Household: Spells & Rituals for the Home*. St. Paul, Minn.: Llewellyn Publications, 2003.

Davies, Owen. *Cunning-folk: Popular Magic in English History*. London: Hambledon and London*, 2002.

———. "Decriminalising the Witch: The Origin of and Response to the 1736 Witchcraft Act." In *Witchcraft and the Act of 1604*, edited by John Newton and Jo Bath, 207–32. Studies in Medieval and Reformation Traditions 131. Leiden; Boston: Brill, 2008.

———. *A People Bewitched: Witchcraft and Magic in Nineteenth-Century Somerset*. Cincinnati: F+W Media, 2012.

———. *Witchcraft, Magic and Culture, 1736-1951*. Manchester: Manchester University Press, 1999.

Davies, Owen, and Timothy Easton. "Cunning-Folk and the Production of Magical Artefacts." In *Physical Evidence for Ritual Acts, Sorcery and Witchcraft in Christian Britain: A Feeling for Magic*, edited by Ronald Hutton, 209–31. Palgrave Historical Studies in Witchcraft and Magic. Houndmills, Basingstoke, Hampshire: Palgrave Macmillan, 2016.

Davis, Daniel Webster. "Folk-Lore and Ethnology: Conjuration." *Southern Workman* 24 (December 1898): 251–52.

Davis, Ralph. *An Account of the Tryals, Examination, and Condemnation, of Elinor Shaw, and Mary Phillip's (Two Notorious Witches), Northampton Assizes, on Wednesday the 7th of March 1705.* London: F. Thorn, 1705.

Dawson, William Harbutt. *History of Skipton: (W.R. Yorks.).* London; Skipton: Simpkin, Marshall; Edmondson, 1882.

De Waardt, Hans. "From Cunning Man to Natural Healer." In *New Perspectives on Witchcraft, Magic, and Demonology 5: Witchcraft, Healing, and Popular Diseases*, edited by Brian P. Levack, 39–47. New York [u.a.: Routledge, 2001.

Dent, J. Geoffrey. "A Yorkshire Witch-Bottle." *Gwerin* 3, no. 4 (1962): 215–17.

Doddridge, Joseph. *Notes on the Settlement and Indian Wars of the Western Parts of Virginia and Pennsylvania, from 1763 to 1783, Inclusive: Together with a View of the State of Society, and Manners of the First Settlers of the Western Country.* Albany, N.Y.: J. Munsell, 1876.

Dominic Winter Auctioneers. "Lot 242 (Printed Books, Maps, Documents, The Library of Patricia Milne-Henderson, Bookbinding Tools, 29th January 2020)." Dominic Winter Auctioneers, January 29, 2020 www.dominicwinter.co.uk/Auction/Lot/242-witchcraft/?lot=355071&sd=1.

Donmoyer, Patrick. *Powwowing in Pennsylvania: Braucherei and the Ritual of Everyday Life.* Kutztown, PA: Pennsylvania German Cultural Heritage Center, 2018.

Drage, William. *Daimonomageia: A Small Treatise of Sicknesses and Diseases from Witchcraft, and Supernatural Causes: Never Before, at Least in This Comprised Order, and General Manner, Was the Like Published: Being Useful to Others besides Physicians, in That It Confutes Atheistical, Sadducistical, and Sceptical Principles and Imaginations.* London: Printed by J. Dover ..., 1665.

Durbin, Henry. *A Narrative of Some Extraordinary Things That Happened to Mr. Richard Giles's Children at the Lamb, without Lawford's-Gate, Bristol: Supposed to be the effect of witchcraft. By the late Mr. Henry Durbin ...* Bristol: R. Edwards, 1800.

E. "Witchcraft in the Present Day: To the Editor of the Times." *Times of London*, April 7, 1857.

Easton, Timothy. "Four Spiritual Middens in Mid Suffolk, England, ca. 1650 to 1850." *Historical Archaeology* 48, no. 3 (2014): 10–34.

Ewen, C. L'Estrange, and Great Britain Courts of Assize and Nisi Prius. *Witch Hunting and Witch Trials: The Indictments for Witchcraft from the Records of 1373 Assizes Held for the Home Circuit A.D. 1559-1736.* New York: Barnes & Noble, 1971.

"Extraordinary Superstition at Plymouth." *Times of London*, November 29, 1843.

Farley, Michael. "A Witch-Bottle from Winslow." *Records of Buckinghamshire* 20, no. 4 (1978): 635–36.

Forby, Robert. *The Vocabulary of East Anglia: An Attempt to Record the Vulgar Tongue of the Twin Sister Counties, Norfolk and Suffolk.*, 1830.

Fowler, James. "On the Process of Decay in Glass, and, Incidentally, on the Composition and Texture of Glass at Different Periods, and the History of Its Manufacture." *Archaeologia: Or, Miscellaneous Tracts Relating to Antiquity, Published by the Society of Antiquaries of London* 46 (1880): 64–162.

Frank C. Brown Collection of North Carolina Folklore., Newman Ivey White, Frank Clyde Brown, and North Carolina Folklore Society. *The Frank C. Brown Collection of North Carolina Folklore; the Folklore of North Carolina, Collected by Dr. Frank C. Brown during the Years 1912 to 1943, in Collaboration with the North Carolina Folklore Society.* Durham, N.C.: Duke University Press, 1952.

"Fulbourn Man's Superstition: Twentieth Century 'Witchcraft.'" *Cambridge Independent Press*, February 6, 1903.

Furie, Michael. *Supermarket Sabbats: A Magical Year Using Everyday Ingredients.* Woodbury, MN: Llewellyn, 2017.

Gårdbäck, Johannes Björn. *Trolldom: Spells and Methods of the Norse Folk Magic Tradition.* Forestville, CA: Yronwode Institution for the Preservation and Popularization of Indigenous Ethnomagicology, 2015.

Gary, Gemma. *Wisht Waters: Aqueous Magica and the Cult of Holy Wells.* Three Hands Press Occult Monographs 5. Richmond Vista, CA: Three Hands Press, 2014.

Gaskill, Malcolm. "The Fear and Loathing of Witches." In *Spellbound: Magic, Ritual, and Witchcraft*, edited by Sophie Page, Marina Wallace, Owen Davies, Malcolm Gaskill, and Ceri Houlbrook, 97–141. Oxford: Ashmolean Museum, 2018.

Gibson, Erica. "Crosses and Witch Bottles." In *Putting the "There" There: Historical Archaeologies of West Oakland*, edited by Mary Praetzellis and Adrian Praetzellis, 182. Rohnert Park, CA: Anthropological Studies Center, 2004.

Gifford, George, Richard Field, Charles Finney Cox, Arthur Johnson, and Felix Kingston. *A Dialogue Concerning Witches and Witchcraft: In Which Is Layed Open How Craftily the Diuell Deceiueth Not Onely the Witches, but Many Other, and So Leadeth Them Awrie into Manie Great Errours.* London: Printed by R.F. and F.K. and are to be sold by Arthur Iohnson, 1603.

Glanvil, Joseph. *Saducismus Triumphatus: Or, Full and Plain Evidence Concerning Witches and Apparitions.* London: Printed for J. Collins at his shop under the Temple Church, and S. Lounds at, 1681.

Glyde, John. *The Norfolk Garland: A Collection of the Superstitious Beliefs and Practices, Proverbs, Curious Customs, Ballads and Songs of the People of Norfolk, as Well as Anecdotes Illustrative of the Genious or Peculiarities of Norfolk Celebrities.* London: Jarrold and Sons, 1872.

Godbeer, Richard. *The Devil's Dominion: Magic and Religion in Early New England.* Cambridge [England]; New York: Cambridge University Press, 1992.

Golding, Ryan. *Tales of Churel: Dead Water.* Dalewood Productions, 2017.

Great Britain, Court of Oyer and Terminer and Gaol Delivery (London and Middlesex). *A Full and True Account of the Proceedings at the Sessions of Oyer and Terminer, Holden for the City of London, County of Middlesex, and Goal-Delivery [sic] of Newgate Which Began at the Sessions-House in the Old-Bayly, on Thursday, Iune 1st, and Ended on Fryday, Iune 2d, 1682: Wherein Is Contained the Tryal of Many Notorious Malefactors, for Murders, Fellonies, Burglary, and Other Misdemeanors, but More Especially the Tryal of Jane Kent for Witchcraft ...* [London?]: Printed for T. Benskin, 1682.

Gregor, Walter. "Stories of Fairies from Scotland." *The Folk-Lore Journal* 1, no. 2 (1883): 55–58.

Gruffydd, Eirlys. "Buckley Pot Used in Witchcraft." *Buckley* 6 (1981): 42.

Hall, Carla Lynne. "The Tale of The Civil War Hoodoo Spell Bottle." *Witch with Me* (blog), February 25, 2020. https://witchwithme.com/2020/02/25/the-tale-of-the-civil-war-hoodoo-spell-bottle/.

Hänselmann, Ludwig. "Die Vergrabenen und Eingemauerten Thongeschirre des Mittelalters." *Westermanns Monatshefte* 41 (77 1876): 393–405.

Harms, Dan, and S. Aldarnay. *The Book of Four Wizards*. Woodbury, MN: Llewellyn Publications, Forthcoming.

Haselgrove, Dennis. "Imported Pottery in the 'Book of Rates": English Customs Categories in the 16th and 17th Centuries." In *Everyday and Exotic Pottery from Europe: C. 650-1900 ; Studies in Honor of John G. Hurst*, edited by David R. M. Gaimster and John G. Hurst, 324–35. Oxford: Oxbow Books, 1992.

Henningsen, Gustav. "Witchcraft Persecution after the Era of the Witch Trials: A Contribution to Danish Ethnohistory." In *New Perspectives on Witchcraft, Magic, and Demonology 6: Witchcraft in the Modern World*, edited by Brian P. Levack, 163–213. New York [u.a.: Routledge, 2001.

Hewett, Sarah. *Nummits and Crummits: Devonshire Customs, Characteristics, and Folk-lore*. Norwood, Pa.: Norwood Editions, 1973.

Hinds, Katie. "Record ID: WILT-71DA46 - POST MEDIEVAL Stopper." *Portable Antiquities Scheme*, July 1, 2009. http://finds.org.uk/database/artefacts/record/id/262693.

———. "Record ID: WILT-F46577 - MEDIEVAL Stopper." *Portable Antiquities Scheme*, July 1, 2006. http://finds.org.uk/database/artefacts/record/id/138424.

Hockley, Frederick, and Silens Manus. *Occult Spells: A Nineteenth Century Grimoire*. York Beach, ME: The Teitan Press, 2009.

Hoggard, Brian. "The Archaeology of Counter-witchcraft and Popular Magic." In *Beyond the Witch Trials: Witchcraft and Magic in Enlightenment Europe*, 167–186. Manchester: Manchester University Press, 2004.

———. "The Archaeology of Folk Magic." *White Dragon*, 1999.

———. *Magical House Protection: The Archaeology of Counter-Witchcraft*. New York: Berghahn, 2019.

———. "Witch Bottles: Their Contents, Contexts and Uses." In *Physical Evidence for Ritual Acts, Sorcery and Witchcraft in Christian Britain: A Feeling for Magic*, edited by Ronald Hutton, 91–105. Palgrave Historical Studies in Witchcraft and Magic. Houndmills, Basingstoke, Hampshire: Palgrave Macmillan, 2016.

Hohman, Johann Georg, and Daniel Harms. *The Long-Lost Friend: A 19th Century American Grimoire*. Woodbury, Minn: Llewellyn Publications, 2012.

Holmes, M. R. "The So-Called 'Bellarmine' Mask on Imported Rhenish Stoneware." *The Antiquaries Journal* 31 (1951): 173–9.

Hope, Robert Charles. *The Legendary Lore of the Holy Wells of England: Including Rivers, Lakes, Fountains, and Springs*. London: Elliot Stock, 1893.

Howard, Michael. *East Anglian Witches and Wizards*. Witchcraft in the British Isles 4. [n. p.]: Three Hands Press, 2017.

Hughes, Vic. "Shadows." *The Witch's Bottle*. ITV, September 17, 1975.

Hunt, Robert. *Popular Romances of the West of England: Or, the Drolls, Traditions, and Superstitions of Old Cornwall*. London: Chatto & Windus, 1908.

———. *Popular Romances of the West of England: Or, the Drolls, Traditions, and Superstitions of Old Cornwall Ser. 2 [...]*. London: Hotten, 1865.

Hyatt, Harry Middleton. *Folk-lore from Adams County, Illinois*. [N.p., 1965.

———. *Hoodoo--Conjuration--Witchcraft--Rootwork; Beliefs Accepted by Many Negroes and White Persons, These Being Orally Recorded Among Blacks and Whites*. Hannibal, Mo.: Printed by Western Pub.; distributed by American University Bookstore, Washington, 1970.

Iafrate, Allegra. *The Long Life of Magical Objects: A Study in the Solomonic Tradition*. University Park, PA: The Pennsylvania State University Press, 2019.

Jeffries, Nigel. "What Should You Do If You Find a 17th-Century 'Witch Bottle'?" Museum of London Archaeology, April 16, 2019. www.mola.org.uk/blog/what-should-you-do-if-you-find-17th-century-witch-bottle.

Kelly, P. "Witch Bottles." *Chemistry in Britain* 36, no. 2 (2000): 56.

Kelway, A. Clifton. *Memorials of Old Essex*. London: George Allen & Sons, 1908.

Kent Archaeological Society. "Investigations and Excavations during the Year." *Archaeologia Cantiana* 83 (1968): 249–51.

King, Julia A. "The Patuxent Point Site." In *Living and Dying on the 17th Century Patuxent Frontier*, edited by Julia A. King and Douglas H. Ubelaker, 15–46. Crownsville, MD: The Maryland Historical Trust Press, 1996.

King, P. M., and A. Massey. "A Miniature Witch Bottle?" *Current Archaeology* 197 (2005): 214–15.

Kingsley, Charles. *At Last: A Christmas in the West Indies*. London: Macmillan and Co., 1896.

Lamont, Jessica L. "The Curious Case of the Cursed Chicken: A New Binding Ritual from the Athenian Agora." *Hesperia: The Journal of the American School of Classical Studies at Athens* 90, no. 1 (2021): 79–113.

Latham, Charlotte. "Some West Sussex Superstitions Lingering in 1868." *The Folk-Lore Record* 1 (1878): 1–67.

Lawson, Deodat. *Christ's Fidelity, The Only Shield against Satan's Malignity. Asserted in a Sermon Delivered at Salem-Village, the 24th of March, 1692, Being Lecture-Day There, and a Time of Publick Examination, of Some Suspected for WITCHCRAFT*. Boston: B. Harris, 1693.

Lewis, Hana. "From Prehistoric to Urban Shoreditch: Excavations at Holywell Priory, Holywell Lane, London EC2." *London Archaeologist* 12, no. 9 (2010): 249–54.

Little, William. *The History of Warren: A Mountain Hamlet, Located Among the White Hills of New Hampshire*. Manchester, N.H.: W. E. Moore, 1870.

Longman, E. D., and S. Loch. *Pins and Pincushions*. London: Longmans, Green and Co., 1911.

Maloney, Catherine. "Witch Bottle from Dukes Place, Aldgate." *Transactions of the London and Middlesex Archaeological Society* 31 (1980): 157–58.

Manning, M. Chris. "Buried Bottles: The Archaeology of Witchcraft and Sympathetic Magic." Poster, 2011.

———. "Homemade Magic: Concealed Deposits in Architectural Contexts in the Eastern United States." Masters' thesis, Ball State University, 2012.

———. "The Material Culture of Ritual Concealments in the United States." *Historical Archaeology* 48, no. 3 (2014): 52–83.

Maple, Eric. *The Dark World of Witches.* New York: A.S. Barnes, 1964.

"Martha Emerson." Salem Witch Trials Documentary Archive and Transcription Project, 2002. http://salem.lib.virginia.edu/texts/tei/BoySal1R?div_id=n47.

Massey, Alan. "Field Note." *Archaeology*, 2002.

———. *Witch Bottle Magic.* n.p.: Privately Published, 2017. (not consulted)

Massey, Alan, and Tony Edmonds. "The Reigate Witch Bottle." *Current Archaeology* 169 (2000): 34–6.

Massey, Alan G., Roger Smith, and Timothy Smith. "A Witch Bottle from Dorset." *Education in Chemistry* 40 (2003): 97–100.

Mather, Cotton, and Richard Baxter. *Late Memorable Providences Relating to Witchcrafts and Possessions Clearly Manifesting, Not Only That There Are Witches, but That Good Men (as Well as Others) May Possibly Have Their Lives Shortned by Such Evil Instruments of Satan.* London: Printed for Tho. Parkhurst ..., 1691.

Mather, Increase. *A Further Account of the Tryals of the New-England Witches with the Observations of a Person Who Was upon the Place Several Days When the Suspected Witches Were First Taken into Examination: To Which Is Added, Cases of Conscience Concerning Witchcrafts and Evil Spirits Personating Men.* London: Printed for J. Dunton ..., 1693.

———. *An Essay for the Recording of Illustrious Providences, Wherein an Account Is Given of Many Remarkable and Very Memorable Events, which Have Happened in This Last Age; Especially in New-England = Remarkable Providences.* Printed at Boston in New-England: and are to be sold by George Calvert at the sign of the Half-moon in Pauls Church-yard, London, 1684.

Merrifield, Ralph. *The Archaeology of Ritual and Magic.* New York: New Amsterdam, 1988.

———. "The Use of Bellarmines as Witch-Bottles." *The Guildhall Miscellany* 3 (1954): 3–15.

———. "Witch Bottles and Magical Jugs." *Folklore* 66, no. 1 (1955): 195–207.

Merrifield, Ralph, and Norman Smedley. "Two Witch-bottles from Suffolk." *Proceedings of the Suffolk Institute of Archaeology* 28, no. 1 (1958): 97–100.

MJD, and Pitt Rivers Museum. "1926.6.1: Glass Flask Reputed to Contain a Witch." Pitt Rivers Museum, June 19, 2013. http://objects.prm.ox.ac.uk/pages/PRMUID25731.html.

Moore, Ruby Andrews. "Superstitions in Georgia." *The Journal of American Folklore* 5, no. 18 (July 1, 1892): 230–31.

Morehouse, Rebecca. "Curator's Choice: Witch Bottle." *Maryland Department of Planning Jefferson Patterson Park and Museum*, 2009. www.jefpat.org/CuratorsChoiceArchive/2009CuratorsChoice/Aug2009-WitchBottle.html.

Morrison, Arthur, and Eric Maple. *Marsh Wizards, Witches and Cunning Men: A Study of Cunning Murrell, George Pickingill, and Witchcraft in 19th Century Essex.* Burbage: Caduceus Books, 2008.

Mulvihill, Mary. "Dublin's Weird 'Witch' Bottle." *Ingenious Ireland*, November 6, 2012. http://ingeniousireland.ie/2012/11/dublins-weird-witch-bottle/.

Museum of Witchcraft and Magic. "14 - Witch Bottle: Bellarmine Jar." Museum of Witchcraft and Magic, 2018. https://museumofwitchcraftandmagic.co.uk/object/witch-bottle-bellarmine-jar/.

———. "221 - Witch Bottle: Bellarmine Jar." Museum of Witchcraft and Magic, 2018. https://museumofwitchcraftandmagic.co.uk/object/witch-bottle-bellarmine-jar-2/.

———. "1438 - Witch Bottle." Museum of Witchcraft and Magic, 2018. https://museumofwitchcraftandmagic.co.uk/object/bottle-14/.

———. "1830 - Spirit Bottle: Witch Bottle." Museum of Witchcraft and Magic, 2018. https://museumofwitchcraftandmagic.co.uk/object/spirit-bottle-witch-bottle-2/.

Nicholson, Isaac. *A Sermon Against Witchcraft: Preached in the Parish Church of Great Paxton, in the County of Huntingdon, July 17, 1808. With a Brief Account of the Circumstances which Led to Two Atrocious Attacks on the Person of Ann Izzard, as a Reputed Witch*. London: Printed for J. Mawman, 1808.

Orser, Charles E. "Rethinking 'Bellarmine' Contexts in 17th-Century England." *Post-Medieval Archaeology* 53, no. 1 (June 2019): 88–101.

Ossman, and Steel. *The Guide to Health or Household Instructor*. Wiconisco, Pa.: Ossman & Steel, 1894.

Owles, Elizabeth, and Norman Smedley. "Archaeology in Suffolk, 1962." *Proceedings of the Suffolk Institute of Archaeology* 29, no. 2 (1962): 166–74.

P., E. "Witchcraft in North Devon." *North Devon Journal*, August 10, 1876.

P., T. *Cas Gan Gythraul: Demonology, Witchcraft, and Popular Magic in Eighteenth-Century Wales*. Edited by South Wales Record Society. Translated by Lisa Tallis. Publications of the South Wales Record Society 28. Newport: South Wales Record Society, 2015.

Painter, F. "An Early 18th Century Witch Bottle: A Legacy of the Wicked Witch of Pungo." *The Chesopeian* 18, no. 3–6 (1980): 62–71.

Parsons, Catherine E. "Notes on Cambridgeshire Witchcraft." *Proceedings of the Cambridge Antiquarian Society, with Communications Made to the Society*. 19 (1914): 31–49.

Peacock, Edward. *A Glossary of Words Used in the Wapentakes of Manley and Corringham, Lincolnshire*. London: Pub. for the English dialect Society by Trübner & Co., 1877.

———. "Replies: Easter Sunday Superstitions." *Notes and Queries* 2nd S. 1, no. 21 (1856): 415.

Peacock, Mabel. "The Folklore of Lincolnshire." *Folklore* 12, no. 2 (June 1, 1901): 161–180.

Pennick, Nigel. *Skulls, Cats, and Witch Bottles*. Bar Hill, Cambridge: Nigel Pennick Editions, 1986.

Perrin, William Henry. *History of Alexander, Union and Pulaski Counties, Illinois*. Chicago, Ill.: O.L. Baskin & Co., 1883.

Pestronk, Alan. "The First Neurology Book: De Cerebri Morbis... (1549) by Jason Pratensis." *Archives of Neurology* 45, no. 3 (1988): 341–44.

Pitts, Mike. "Urine to Navel Fluff: The First Complete Witch Bottle." *British Archaeology* no. 107 (2009): n. p.

Powell, Nicky. "The Holywell Witch Bottle." *Museum of London - The Holywell Witch Bottle*, 2008. www.museumoflondonarchaeology.org.uk/NewsProjects/Archive/News08/witchbottle.htm.

Pratensis, Jason. *De Cerebri Morbis: Hoc Est, Omnibus Fermè (Quoniam à Cerebro Male Affecto Omnes Ferè qui Corpus Humanum Infestant, Morbi Oriuntur) Curandis Liber ... Secundum Veterum Graecorum, Latinorum, & Arabum, necnon Recentium Praecepta, Magno Iudicio & Arte Conscriptus, & Nunc Primùm in Lucem Aeditus ...* Basileae: Henricum Petri, 1549.

"Provincial Intelligence." *Lloyd's Weekly Newspaper*. London, April 1, 1849.

Puckett, Newbell Niles. "Folk Beliefs of the Southern Negro." University of North Carolina Press; H. Milford, 1926.

Raine, Kathleen. *Depositions from the Castle of York, Relating to Offences Committed in the Northern Counties in the Seventeenth Century*. Durham Surtees Society Publications 40. Durham: Frances Andrews, 1861.

Rawlence, E. A. "Sundry Folk-lore Reminiscences Relating to Man and Beast in Dorset and the Neighbouring Counties." *Proceedings of the Dorset Natural History and Antiquarian Field Club* 37 (1916): 56–65.

Reeves, Matthew. "Mundane or Spiritual?: The Interpretation of Glass Bottle Containers Found on Two Sites of the African Diaspora." In *Materialities of Ritual in the Black Atlantic*, edited by Akinwumi Ogundiran and Paula Sanders, 176–97. Bloomington, IN: Indiana University Press, 2014.

Rieti, Barbara. *Making Witches: Newfoundland Traditions of Spells and Counterspells*. Montreal: McGill-Queen's University Press, 2008.

Rose, H. J. "Canadian Folklore." *Folklore* 32, no. 2 (1921): 124–131.

Scot, Reginald. *The Discouerie of Witchcraft: Wherein the Lewde Dealing of Witches and Witchmongers Is Notablie Detected, the Knauerie of Coniurors, the Impietie of Inchantors, the Follie of Soothsaiers, the Impudent Falshood of Cousenors, the Infidelitie of Atheists, the Pestilent Practices of Pythonists, the Curiositie of Figure Casters, the Vanitie of Dreamers, the Beggerlie Art of Alcumystrie, the Abhomination of Idolatrie, the Horrible Art of Poisoning, the Vertue and Power of Naturall Magike, and All the Conueiances of Legierdemaine and Iuggling Are Deciphered: And Many Other Things Opened, Which Have Long Lien Hidden, Howbeit Verie Necessarie to Be Knowne: Heerevnto Is Added a Treatise Vpon the Nature and Substance of Spirits and Diuels, &c.* London: William Brome, 1584.

Semmens, Jason. "The Usage of Witch-bottles and Apotropaic Charms in Cornwall." *Old Cornwall* 12, no. 6 (2000): 25–30.

Smedley, Norman. "Two Bellarmine Bottles from Coddenham." *Proceedings of the Suffolk Institute of Archaeology* 29, no. 3 (1954): 229–30.

Smedley, Norman, Elizabeth Owles, and F. R. Paulsen. "More Suffolk Witch-Bottles." *Proceedings of the Suffolk Institute of Archaeology* 30, no. 1 (1964): 84–92.

Streeten, A. D. F. "Researches and Discoveries in Kent: A 'Bellarmine' Bottle from Hook Green, Lamberhurst." *Archaeologia Cantiana* 92 (1976): 227–28.

Sumnall, Kate. "Record ID: LON-B416A6 - POST MEDIEVAL Bottle." *Portable Antiquities Scheme*, January 1, 1982. http://finds.org.uk/database/artefacts/record/id/159258.

"Superstition in Langport." *Wells Journal*, February 10, 1855.

Sydney, W. C. *The Early Days of the Nineteenth Century in England, 1800-1820*. G. Redway, 1898.

Tannenbaum, Rebecca J. *The Healer's Calling: Women and Medicine in Early New England*. Ithaca, N.Y.: Cornell University Press, 2009.

Thwaite, Ann-Sophie. "Magic and the Material Culture of Healing in Early Modern England." Thesis, Pembroke College, University of Cambridge, 2020.

Thwaite, Annie. "What Is a 'Witch Bottle'?: Assembling the Textual Evidence from Early Modern England." *Magic, Ritual, and Witchcraft* 15, no. 2 (2020): 227–51.

Tilley, Ernest. "A Witch-bottle from Gravesend." *Archaeologia Cantiana* 80 (1965): 252–8.

TipToeChick. "How to Make a Witch Bottle." *YouTube*, April 18, 2012. www.youtube.com/watch?v=crnk00ChBpg.

Tryon, Thomas. *The Way to Save Wealth; Shewing How a Man May Live Plentifully for Two Pence a Day*. London: G. Conyers, 1695.

Walker, John. "A Witch Bottle from Hellington." *Norfolk Archaeology* 40 (1987): 113–14.

Waters, Thomas E. *Cursed Britain: A History of Witchcraft and Black Magic in Modern Times*. New Haven, CT: Yale University Press, 2019.

Weinstein, M. *Earth Magic: A Book of Shadows for Positive Witches*. New Page Books, 2003.

Wellacott, W. T. "A Churchyard Charm." *Report and Transactions of the Devonshire Association for the Advancement of Science, Literature and Art* 28 (1895): 98–99.

Wheeler, Sophie, and Jordan Coussins. "Man Spooked after Unearthing Witch Bottle Containing Hair, Urine and Human Tooth." BirminghamLive, July 5, 2021. www.birminghammail.co.uk/black-country/man-spooked-after-unearthing-witch-20970110.

Wheeler, Walter. "Magical Dwelling: Apotropaic Building Practices in the New World Dutch Cultural Hearth." In *Religion, Cults, and Rituals in the Medieval Rural Environment*, edited by Claudia Theune and Christiane Bis-Worch, 373–96. Ruralia 11. Leiden: Sidestone Press, 2017.

White, Andrew. "Witch Bottle with a Halloween Link Is Object of the Week." *The Northern Echo*, October 26, 2019. www.thenorthernecho.co.uk/news/17991352.witch-bottle-halloween-link-object-week.

Whitley, H. Michell. "Cornish Folklore: To Avert an Ill Wish." *Devon and Cornwall Notes and Queries* 11 (1921): 288.

Whitney, Annie Weston, and Caroline Canfield Bullock. *Folk-lore from Maryland,*. New York: American Folk-lore Society, 1925.

Wilkie, Laurie A. "Secret and Sacred: Contextualizing the Artifacts of African-American Magic and Religion." *Historical Archaeology* 31, no. 4 (1997): 81–106.

Wilkinson, Tattersall. "Local Folk Lore." *Papers, Reports, &c., Read Before the Halifax Antiquarian Society*. (1904): 2–9.

"'Witchcraft' at Chesterfield: Palmistry, Charms, and Dragon's Blood." *Derbyshire Times and Chesterfield Herald*, October 17, 1888.

"Witchcraft in Stockport." *Belfast Daily Mercury*, November 23, 1857.

Yamin, Rebecca., New Jersey Department of Transportation., and Federal Highway Administration. *Rediscovering Raritan Landing: An Adventure in New Jersey Archaeology*, 2011.

Yamin, Rebecca, and Donna J. Seifert. *The Archaeology of Prostitution and Clandestine Pursuits*. Gainesville: University Press of Florida, 2019.

Yronwode, Catherine. "Witch Bottles: Hoodoo and British." *Witch Bottles: Hoodoo and British*, 2000. http://sonic.net/~yronwode/arcane-archive.org/occultism/magic/folk/hoodoo/witch-bottles-hoodoo-and-british-1.php.

———. "Witch's Bottle (Malevolent, Not Protective)." *Witch's Bottle*, 1999. www.arcane-archive.org/occultism/magic/folk/hoodoo/witch-bottle-1.php.

Index

A

Aberdeenshire 61
Accomac 75
Alabama 78, 103
Alsace 71
amulets 24, 32
animals 18, 23, 50, 68
apotropaic 16, 94
Arts and Humanities Research Council 99
ash, wood 29, 32, 33
Athens 28, 107

B

Bahamas 79
Bailer, Aunt Sophia 73
Barnstaple 59
Bedfordshire 51
Bell, Sir Henry Hesketh Joudou 80
Bellarmine, Robert 36
bellarmines 36, 37, 88, 89
Bellhouse 21, 55, 90, 92, 102
Bible 70
Bishops Stortford 63
Blagrave 14, 39, 40, 41, 55, 89, 93, 102
bleeding 24, 88
blood 12, 17, 24, 32, 40, 51, 52, 54, 55, 56, 70, 72, 84, 87, 90
Bodmin 48, 62
bones 29, 92
Boscastle 5, 62, 83
Bossiney 62
Boston 15, 67, 103, 107, 108
Bottesford 57
bowls 16, 29, 31
Bradford 51
Bradworthy 60
Brearly, William 34
Brierley 18, 59, 102
brimstone 56
Britain 44, 47, 50, 62, 65, 103, 104, 105, 106, 107, 111
Brown, Dr. Frank C. 77, 105
Browne, Ray 78
Brushy Fork 77
Buckley 61, 106
butter 24, 36

C

cabbage 84
Camborne 62
Cambridge 34, 102, 105, 109, 111
Cambridgeshire 63, 83, 109
Campbell 60, 61, 103
Canewdon 54, 64, 101
Caribbean 79
cat 47, 94
cattle 41, 49, 50, 88
Chesterfield 59, 111
chicken 28, 76, 83
chimney .37, 43, 49, 54, 56, 63, 74, 78, 88, 96
Choppen the smith 52
churchyard 48, 60, 65
coins 28, 29, 85
Cologne 36
Colonie 71
Columbia 75
conjure 42, 75, 77, 78, 79, 95
Copenhagen 65, 102
Cornish 18, 50, 62, 96, 111
Cornwall 41, 51, 61, 62, 83, 88, 102, 107, 110, 111
cotinine 39
Crewkerne 58
crossroads 18, 62
Crowther, Timothy 32
Culliford 58, 59
Cunningham, Scott 84

113

D

Daimonomageia 36, 104
dandelion 84
Davies, Owen 52, 105
Davis, David Webster 76
Dawson Bellhouse, William 14, 21, 54
De Cerebri Morbis 33, 34, 109, 110
Delaware 71, 74, 102
Denmark 65
Der Lange Verborgene Freund 71
Devon 63, 109, 111
Discoverie of Witchcraft 34
divination 51, 75
Doddridge, Joseph 74
doll 57
donkey 53
Dorset 49, 64, 95, 103, 108, 110
Drage, William 36, 90
dragon's blood 54
dragonsblood 17
dung 54, 61

E

East Anglia 38, 52, 95, 104
Eliot 70
Emerson, Martha 15, 68, 69, 108
England ... 4, 14, 19, 34, 36, 37, 45, 51, 56, 62, 65, 67, 68, 88, 91, 97, 101, 103, 104, 105, 106, 107, 108, 109, 111
epilepsy 57
erotic 18
Essex 24, 52, 63, 64, 88, 101, 107, 108
Essington 71
evil spirits 29, 42
Exeter 63

F

faeces 84
Farrar, Stewart 86
Fayette County 78
Fernee, Ben 5, 21
fingernail 49, 56, 71, 74
fishhooks 56
Foot, Emma 58

foundation sacrifices 29
Fowler, James 65
frog 60, 61
funerary offerings 28

G

galvanist 14, 54
Gardner, Gerald 82
Gary, Gemma 83
Georgia 78, 108
German 5, 71, 72, 74, 79, 96, 104
Germany 16, 29, 32
Gifford, Reverend George 31
Glanvil 36, 61, 94, 105
Glanvil, Joseph 34
good fortune 29
Gospel of St. John 30
Governor Printz State Park 71
graveyard dirt 84
Great Island 69, 103
Great Paxton 51, 109
Greene, Ann 32
Grenada 80
grimoire 21
Gudbrandsdalen 65
Guildford 57

H

Hadleigh 52
hair .. 16, 32, 38, 39, 44, 45, 49, 51, 52, 53, 54, 55, 56, 57, 58, 60, 63, 65, 68, 70, 74, 80, 90
Hale, Mary 67
Halifax 70, 111
Harrington, David 84, 103
Haynes, Lilian 59
headache 32
healer 32, 67, 73
healing 15, 65, 73
heart 58, 59,88, 91, 92
  animal 16, 17, 18, 24, 29, 30, 32, 33, 38, 39, 43, 52, 54, 55, 57, 72, 93
  cloth 30
  felt 38, 74

toad 60
witch 57, 59, 95
Helston 62
herbs 24, 80, 85, 92
Highway, Ted 60
Hill, Ann. Agnes 32
Hockham 58
Hoggard, Brian 89
Hohman, John George 71
Holland 34
Holyhead 61
Holywood 56
hoodoo 75, 77, 84, 106, 112
Horn, Charlotte 32
horsehair 78
Horseheath 63
horses 18, 47
horseshoe 33, 58
horseshoes 24, 39, 52
hot foot powder 84
Hove 82
Hudson Valley 71
Hunt, Robert 62
Hyatt, Harry Middleton 77

I

Illinois 78, 79, 107, 109
insoles 74
Iowa 79, 95
Ireland 45, 89, 109

J

Jamaica 80
Jones, Louisa 60

K

Kentucky 78
King of the Witches 64
Kingsley, Charles 81
Kingston Lisle 34

L

Langford 58
Langston, Chris 57
Larsen, Jørgen 14, 65

Lawson, Deodat 15, 68
Leeds 54
Leekfrith 60
Liverpool 21, 39, 54
Lord's Prayer 31, 60
Loughborough University 39

M

Maine 70
Manning, Dr. 92
Maple, Eric 64, 108
Margaret Murray 82
Maryland 74, 75, 95, 107, 108, 111
Massey, Alan 39
Mather, Increase 15, 67
Matthew Reeves 80
Merrifield, Ralph 26
Merrill, Stevens 70
Middle East 29
milk 36, 55, 60, 61, 88
Monkleigh Parish 63
Morrison, Arthur 52
Murrell, James 'Cunning' 52
Museum of London Archaeology .. 99, 107
Museum of Witchcraft and Magic ... 5, 83, 109

N

nails. 16, 25, 31, 32, 33, 38, 40, 41, 43, 49, 52, 54, 55, 58, 63, 68, 70, 71, 75, 76, 78, 80, 81, 84, 86, 87, 90, 93
doornail 28
fingernails 39, 47, 65
Nanny Roberts 61
needles ... 16, 25, 29, 30, 32, 35, 39, 40, 43, 45, 54, 55, 56, 59, 60, 66, 73, 75, 76, 79, 80, 84, 90, 93, 95
Netherlands 16, 29, 37
New Deer 61
New Hampshire 69, 70, 107
Newfoundland 69, 110
Nicholson, Isaac 51
Norfolk ... 33, 43, 45, 58, 88, 104, 105,

111

Nørre Lyndelse 14, 65
North Carolina 77, 105, 110
North Devon 59, 60, 63, 109
North Devon Journal 59, 109
Northampton 31, 45, 68, 104
Northamptonshire 56, 103
Norway 65

O

Obeah 80, 81, 102
Old Henry 77
Ossman and Steel 72, 73
Oswestry 57
ox 57, 108
Oxford 82, 105, 106

P

Padstow 62
Pagan 82, 84
Paracelsian 14, 16, 29, 43, 45
Peacock, Edward 57
Pennick, Nigel 83, 109
Pennsylvania . 5, 15, 71, 72, 73, 74, 75, 96, 101, 102, 104, 107
pentagram 70
Pickingill, George 64, 108
pins . 11, 13, 16, 17, 18, 24, 25, 31, 32, 38, 39, 40, 43, 45, 47, 48, 49, 51, 52, 54, 55, 56, 57, 58, 59, 60, 61, 62, 63, 64, 66, 69, 71, 73, 74, 75, 76, 77, 78, 79, 84, 88, 90, 91, 93, 95
Pistol 35
Pitt Rivers Museum 82, 96, 108
Pittsburgh 74, 101
Plymouth 32, 33, 104
Plymstock 32
powwower 73
Pratensis, Jason 33, 109
Pritchard, Mary Jane 60
Proctor 78
Providence 71
Psalm 55, 58
Pulborough 57

R

Raitt Homestead Farm Museum 70
Ram Mark Pond 55
Rayleigh 53
Rhine valley 72
Rhode Island 71
Rhule, Linton 80
Rieti, Barbara 69
Romany 53
rosemary 84, 85, 86

S

Saducismus Triumphatus ..34, 36, 105
Saffron Walden 5, 24, 101
    Museum 5, 101
Salem 15, 68, 85, 107, 108
salt 17, 40, 41, 55, 85, 92
Salt 40
Saratoga, Witch of 56
Satan 40, 59, 107, 108
Savannah 78
Scandinavia 14, 65
Schuyler family, ... 71
Scot, Reginald 34
Scotland 60, 61, 89, 103, 105
semen 84
Sennen 62
Shadows 86, 106, 111
Shropshire 57
Sloane 3846 .... 41, 42, 93
Smith, Mary Ann 60
Smith, Michael 67
Smith, Simeon 70
Somerset 52, 103
spirit 25, 33, 42, 47, 51, 52, 82, 95, 109
St. Augustine 63
St. Merryn 41, 49, 61
Staffordshire 60, 102
Star and Garter Inn 56
Stephens, Professor George 65
Stockport 56, 111
sulfur 30, 39
Sussex 57, 64, 82, 88, 101, 107
Sutcliffe 51

T

Taylors 71
teeth 17, 54, 56
Tetragrammaton 31
The Love Witch 86, 102
The Strand 52
thorns 11, 16, 25, 38, 45, 52, 58, 60, 90
thresholds 16, 18, 29
Thwaite 29, 37, 45, 90, 91, 94, 111
Tintagel 61
toenails 65
Tournai 34
Tremont 73
Tresmeer 62
Trevone 62
Tubbs, Angeline 56
Tull, Zippy 75

U

Uganda 80
University of Hertfordshire 99
urinary 16, 29, 70
urine 11, 12, 13, 14, 16, 17, 25, 26, 29, 30, 32, 33, 36, 39, 40, 41, 42, 44, 45, 46, 47, 48, 49, 50, 52, 56, 57, 58, 60, 61, 64, 65, 66, 67, 69, 70, 72, 73, 74, 77, 78, 80, 84, 85, 86, 87, 88, 90, 93

V

verbena 84
Virginia 75, 76, 104

W

Wales 61, 89, 109
Walton, George 69
Warren 70, 107
wart 62, 96
Washington 77, 107
Watford 56
Watson, Mrs. 53
Weacome, Hannah 15, 67
Wells 52, 91, 105, 106, 110
Wembley 63
West Indies 80, 81, 102, 107
West Oakland 79, 105
West Virginia 74
Westernoff, Adelina 18, 59
Wicca 82, 84
Wiconisco 72, 109
Williamson, Cecil 83
Wilmington 77
Witch of Pungo 76
witch trials 15, 23, 24, 26, 44
Wood, Deborah 18, 59

Y

Yaddlethorpe 57, 95
Yeovil 55
York 5, 32, 56, 71, 102, 104, 105, 106, 108, 110, 111

Z

Zennor 14, 50, 61
Zierikzee 34

www.avaloniabooks.com

www.ingramcontent.com/pod-product-compliance
Lightning Source LLC
Chambersburg PA
CBHW020358170426
43200CB00005B/222